# HEARERS OF THE
# WORD

## PRAYING & EXPLORING THE READINGS
## EASTER & PENTECOST YEAR C

KIERAN J O'MAHONY OSA

Published by Messenger Publications, 2022

ISBN 9781788124614

Designed by Messenger Publications Design Department
Cover Images: Thoom/Shutterstock
Typeset in adobe Caslon Pro and Adobe Bitter
Printed by Hussar Books

Messenger Publications,
37 Leeson Place, Dublin D02 E5V0
www.messenger.ie

# Antiphon for the Holy Spirit

The Spirit of God
is a life that bestows life,
root of world-tree
and wind in its boughs.

Scrubbing out sin,
she rubs oil into wounds.

She is glistening life
alluring all praise,
all-awakening,
all-resurrecting.


Hildegard of Bingen

For Lonan and Phil

And all the people went up following him,
playing on pipes and rejoicing with great joy,
so that the earth quaked at their noise.
*(1 Kings 1:40)*

# Table of Contents

# Introduction

When I think of Church, an image frequently comes to mind, that of a beached whale. To stay alive at all, it will need constant watering; to get back into the ocean is going to take enormous leverage and some time. Not everyone thinks this is a worthwhile project. The perception of Church as institution can be arrestingly negative: abusive, misogynist, homophobic, money-grabbing, power-seeking. All things the opposite of what Jesus dreamed. What has happened to the word of life, Gospel joy, the great spiritual tradition, the wisdom and guidance we need to live life in abundance? What has become of the 'great events that give us new life in Christ'? What has happened to the outpouring of the Spirit?

It is all still there – immortal diamond! – but difficult to access, camouflaged, not to say concealed, by the weight of history and tradition, custom and sheer apathy. That is why the synodal pathway, proposed and enacted by Pope Francis, is potentially so significant. Consulting all 1.2 billion (nominal) Catholics is a venture never undertaken before. It is a vast venture and potentially a great *adventure*. It is also risky, but then again, to do nothing would constitute an even greater risk. The big risk is not that people won't talk – I think they will. The big risk is that those who have been heard will then expect to be listened to. And there is much to hear.

When Jesus criticised the religious leadership of his day, his words were sharp:

> Isaiah prophesied rightly about you hypocrites, as it is written, 'This people honours me with their lips, but their hearts are far from me; in vain do they worship me, teaching human precepts as doctrines.' You abandon the commandment of God and hold to human tradition. (Mark 7:6–8)

ntuition that
mself, it can
Many in our
s and do not
ome kind of
is discipline,
ve and move
The classical
e. It contin-
e past but is
l of stillness,

not live on
uth of God
certainly en-
written word
xperience of
up for me.
ng on in my
ward spiral.
not only a
a sense of
meditation
invites us to
of presence
*tio* for con-

Vhen we do
e bring our
ence. As we
of God can
bservations
ally need a

community

lere we need to distinguish Tradition
wer case. Some traditions are 'period
it not to be held on to for ever. Tra-
:: the teaching about the triune God,
faith, the classical spiritual tradition
cramental life of the Church, and the
tion. As we listen to what the Spirit is
we shall have to ask, which traditions
nulated over the centuries, but which

can direct us: What does God desire
it another way, how can we as a com-
f life, the Gospel, to ourselves and to
to the next question: How should we
es so that we can more truly serve that

at greater vision may help. At the very
e believe God is love. We believe God
iistry and preaching, in the life, death
areth. We believe 'God's love has been
the Holy Spirit that has been given to
e wedding Mass, love is our origin, love
r fulfilment in heaven. We believe this
really know this in our heart of hearts.
re drawn to the light and life of God.
ie spiritual journey. This might seem
he heart are insistent. But we do live in
p our time, busy with what Luke calls
hese too are insistent but can become a
venture to sentient existence, our minds
l. We are constantly being asked to live
he people is now a dull acceptance that
be satisfied with less. But surely we are
gh life? On the contrary!
e hungers of the heart are registered in

restlessness, the vague – and sometimes not so vague –
there is more. In acute cases, such as for Augustine h
lead to emotional, existential and spiritual breakdown.
day experience this unease but do not recognise what it
know where to turn. In response, nothing can replace
practice of meditation, quiet prayer, sitting with God. It
but we are at least engaging with the God in whom we l
and have our being (Acts 17:28). And we are not alone.
spiritual tradition is alive and well and, nowadays, onlir
ues to be nourished by the great spiritual guides from tl
developing and growing in the present. Without this poc
how would any of us cope?

For that journey, we also require nourishment. We d
bread alone but on every word that comes from the m
(Luke 4:4). The revival of sacred reading (*lectio divina*) is
couraging. Ultimately, the word of God is not simply a
on a page but a place of encounter. To it, I bring my e
life, which can provide a foothold in the text, opening
In turn, the unlocked text can shed light on what is goi
life. This two-way illumination simply continues in an u
Done week in, week out, the pilgrim gradually acquire
bank of experience, not only a wisdom to live by, but al
presence, Emmanuel, God with us. The combination o
and *lectio* is, in my mind, essential and life-giving. *Lectio*
conversion and encounter. Meditation provides that sens
(even presence-in-absence), balancing the demands of *le*
tinued conversion and costly discipleship.

It is a good idea to use the Sunday readings for *lectio*.
join with the community of faith for the Lord's Supper,
own lived experience of the text, which makes all the diffe
hear the reading again in the context of worship, the word
speak to us powerfully, refracted through the reactions and
of others. The process simply goes on and then, when I
word of God in my life, I will be ready to hear it.

We do not eat the bread of life alone; we do it as part of the of faith. The richness and discipline of the lectionary is one expression of that, one of the great fruits of the Second Vatican Council. As that council said:

> The treasures of the Bible are to be opened up more lavishly, so that richer fare may be provided for the faithful at the table of God's word. In this way a more representative portion of the holy scriptures will be read to the people in the course of a prescribed number of years (SC 51).

As we learn how to be a synodal Church, that journey of heart – to God, with the word, in the community – will be central. It may be that we need to learn again how to be a community of faith, how to be hearers of the word together, how to pray and to worship as one. Perhaps then we can discover again the one thing necessary (Luke 10:42) and find again the treasure and be able to offer it to our world.

The journey inwards will have to be matched by a journey outwards. For that, we will certainly need new language and new ways. We will find ourselves invited to set aside merely human traditions so the Gospel can stand out again in all its life-giving glory. Like the believers in the Acts of the Apostles, we will struggle to recognise the Spirit, ahead of us, outside our boundaries, surprising us.

Human rights in recent history sprang from the French Revolution and the subsequent industrial revolutions but are now central to Catholic social teaching. Ecumenism began in the churches of the Reformation but is now central to Catholic identity. We may ask, where else has the Spirit been at work? Surely in the growing tolerance for gender variety. Surely in the recognition of the equality of women. Surely in the growing sense that we all inhabit one world and are responsible for each other. Surely in the extraordinary discoveries about our solar system, the universe and the cosmos. To take all this on board is a great adventure – and will enable us to offer the word of life in our time, unhindered like St Paul (Acts 28:31).

We have gone some distance from the beached whale – not to be forgotten – but it is not all about Church. It is much more fundamentally about how to be human today, in the light of God's disclosure through the one human being Jesus of Nazareth and the Spirit of God at work in him and in us.

Thanks once more to Messenger Publications for staying with the project over the last three years, culminating in this ninth volume. I appreciate very much the professionalism and the patience of all involved. As before, the pointers for prayer on the gospel readings are almost all by John Byrne OSA.

# Chapter 1

## Easter Sunday 1C

### Thought for the day

Traditionally, we have found it easy to think of the cross as the measure of God's love for us. Perhaps because of the focus on the cross, we find it more difficult to think of the resurrection as also the love of God, perhaps 'all the more so'! The originality of the Fourth Gospel says it all: the disciple Jesus loved, the head cloth recalling Lazarus (see how much he loved him) and, not least, the great figure of Mary Magdalene (Mary!). In summary, Jesus died and rose again for love of us.

### Prayer

*Loving God, you love us more than we can imagine or take in. Help us to allow ourselves to be so loved by you, that your love may penetrate our hearts, our lives and our loves. We ask this through Jesus, who died and rose for love of us and who lives and reigns for ever and ever. Amen.*

### Gospel

**Jn 20:1** Early on the first day of the week, while it was still dark, Mary Magdalene came to the tomb and saw that the stone had been removed from the tomb. ² So she ran and went to Simon Peter and the other disciple, the one whom Jesus loved, and said to them, 'They have taken the Lord out of the tomb, and we do not know where they have laid him.'

³ Then Peter and the other disciple set out and went toward the tomb. ⁴ The two were running together, but the other disciple outran Peter and reached the tomb first. ⁵ He bent down to look in and saw the linen wrappings lying there, but he did not go in. ⁶ Then Simon Peter came, following him, and went into the tomb. He saw the linen wrappings lying there, ⁷ and the cloth that had been on Jesus' head, not lying with the linen wrappings but rolled up in a place by itself. ⁸ Then the other disciple, who reached the tomb first, also went in, and he saw and believed; ⁹ for as yet they did not understand the scripture, that he must rise from the dead. ¹⁰ Then the disciples returned to their homes.

¹¹ *But Mary stood weeping outside the tomb. As she wept, she bent over to look into the tomb;* ¹² *and she saw two angels in white, sitting where the body of Jesus had been lying, one at the head and the other at the feet.* ¹³ *They said to her, 'Woman, why are you weeping?' She said to them, 'They have taken away my Lord, and I do not know where they have laid him.'* ¹⁴ *When she had said this, she turned around and saw Jesus standing there, but she did not know that it was Jesus.* ¹⁵ *Jesus said to her, 'Woman, why are you weeping? Whom are you looking for?' Supposing him to be the gardener, she said to him, 'Sir, if you have carried him away, tell me where you have laid him, and I will take him away.'* ¹⁶ *Jesus said to her, 'Mary!' She turned and said to him in Hebrew, 'Rabbouni!' (which means Teacher).* ¹⁷ *Jesus said to her, 'Do not hold on to me, because I have not yet ascended to the Father. But go to my brothers and say to them, "I am ascending to my Father and your Father, to my God and your God".'* ¹⁸ *Mary Magdalene went and announced to the disciples, 'I have seen the Lord'; and she told them that he had said these things to her.*

## Initial observations

The Easter appearance narratives vary greatly and are richly theological, usually dealing with issues current at the time of writing. There is a common core, but the writers dispense with 'historical' precision to privilege theological truth.

Today's excerpt in the lectionary stops at verse 9. It is virtually impossible to understand the passage without reading on until verse 18 (included here). I recommend reading the full text, not otherwise heard this year.

## Kind of writing

Technically, this is a theophany, more precisely a 'Christophany', with the usual features of question, encounter, fear and reassurance/relief.

## Old Testament background

> In the beginning when God created the heavens and the earth, the earth was a formless void and darkness covered the face of the deep, while a wind from God swept over the face of the waters. Then God said, 'Let there be light'; and there was light. (Genesis 1:1–4)

## New Testament foreground

It is odd that Mary seems to be absent during vv. 3–10 and that the disciples, whom she alerted, seem to ignore her. It is odd that we are not told she came back with them although we discover that she did. It is odd that the beloved disciple and Peter simply 'went back to their homes' – to do what exactly? These unusual features become tolerable once we realise we are dealing with a core tradition symbolically expanded by the genius who wrote the Fourth Gospel, for didactic and theological purposes.

The Mary Magdalene story would be perfectly coherent on its own, taking vv. 1, 11–18. It would then resemble the Synoptic stories, with a Johannine flavour. So, why has this writer inserted a narrative of Peter's journey to the tomb, with the addition of the Beloved Disciple? In part, I think, to contrast the limits of the institutional (Petrine; see Luke 24:12, 34) with the dynamism of the charismatic (Johannine). In part, to place at the centre of this Easter proclamation an important recollection of the Lazarus story – (a) to contrast the outcomes and (b) to affirm love as the key to God's gift. 'Bending down' and the head cloth link the scenes. Here is the key text:

> Then Jesus, again greatly disturbed, came to the tomb. It was a cave, and a stone was lying against it. Jesus said, 'Take away the stone.' Martha, the sister of the dead man, said to him, 'Lord, already there is a stench because he has been dead four days.' Jesus said to her, 'Did I not tell you that if you believed, you would see the glory of God?' So they took away the stone. And Jesus looked upward and said, 'Father, I thank you for having heard me. I knew that you always hear me, but I have said this for the sake of the crowd standing here, so that they may believe that you sent me.' When he had said this, he cried with a loud voice, 'Lazarus, come out!' The dead man came out, his hands and feet bound with strips of cloth, and his face wrapped in a cloth. Jesus said to them, 'Unbind him, and let him go.' (John 11:38–44)

A component of the gospel writer's objective here is to recount how we come to resurrection faith. This gospel brings something very special for our consideration. Earlier, in John 11, we read that the gift of resurrected life flows from the love of God or the Son of God's distress at the human condition ('Jesus wept'). Correspondingly, the double story here tells us that the move to Easter faith is also a movement of love. The eyes of faith are opened by the heart. Such an analysis explains both the structure of the passage and the oddity of it.

A   vv. 1–3:   Mary on a quest like the early stories in this Gospel

B   vv. 4–10:   Partial resurrection faith: love + scripture

A*   vv. 11–18:   One-to-one encounter completes the quest

## St Paul

So if anyone is in Christ, there is a new creation: everything old has passed away; see, everything has become new! (2 Corinthians 5:17)

## Brief commentary

(V. 1)
First day (cf. Galatians 6:15) echoing creation. Darkness is symbolic, as always in John. Notice the lack of motive and that Mary is alone (but becomes 'we' later) because this gospel prefers one-to-one encounters. The stone is identified as already removed. It was not mentioned in the burial of Jesus in John 19:42.

(V. 2)
Mary communicates with the disciples, contrary to Mark's ending, which underlines the silence of the women. The Beloved Disciple is to be found only in this gospel. This elusive figure may be the original, historical inspiration of the tradition. As portrayed in the text, the Beloved Disciple has become a model for all believers, always faithful in love and the first to come to faith. Notice the logic of the hypothesis: tombs can be empty for various reasons.

(Vv. 3–4)
They run, which is an indication of their eagerness. The Beloved Disciple is quicker, not on account of his physical fitness/youth but because he loves the Lord. In the Johannine tradition, the Beloved Disciple is the hero and model, contrasted with Peter.

(V. 5)
Why did he not go in? At a narrative level, to show deference to Peter,

but also to set up a contrast with Peter, who does enter but does not come to faith as quickly.

(Vv. 6–7)
The details are emphasised and therefore highly significant. In this way, the outcome from this burial is contrasted with that of Lazarus (John 11:44: *The dead man came out, his hands and feet bound with strips of cloth, and his face wrapped in a cloth. Jesus said to them, 'Unbind him, and let him go.'*).

(V.8)
The choreography points to a kind of priority of honour to Peter. Both saw the same 'empirical residue', yet only the one who loved made the leap of faith. 'Seeing' is a verb for faith in this gospel (and sometimes not!).

(V. 9)
The gloss may seem strange, seeing that the Beloved Disciples did come to faith. However, full resurrection faith comes by means of an encounter with the risen Jesus (cf. next scene) and by confirmation in Scripture. In any case, the 'not yet understanding' is a theme right from the start of the Fourth Gospel, sustained even here.

(V. 10)
To do what? The writer brusquely clears the 'stage' for the one-to-one encounter to come. Once again, we are not dealing here with history but with a symbolic narrative.

(V. 11)
Seemingly, there is no contact with the Beloved Disciple and Peter. In an important way, as she peers into the tomb, Mary replicates the initial action of the Beloved Disciple.

(V.12)
Angels indicate that something transcendent has taken place. In the New Testament white is the colour of the resurrection. Again, the head of Jesus is underlined, evoking the veil in John 11. Nothing is by accident

in the Fourth Gospel and so the feet recall anointing in John 12.

(V.13)

'Woman', as an address, is found in Cana (mother), Jacob's well (journey of faith); at the cross (mother) and, finally, here at the resurrection (journey of faith). Mary repeats her 'earthly' grasp of the events, echoing her earlier assessment.

(V. 14)

It is not at all clear why she turned around – at least not yet. It is also usual in resurrection appearance stories that Jesus is not immediately recognised.

(V. 15)

Jesus repeats the words of the angels. There is intense irony (gardener; sir, if, take him away). Mary is still somehow 'outside' the mystery. There is no reason to weep. Jesus' second question takes us back to the first words he speaks in this gospel: 'What are you looking for' (1:38), except 'what' has become 'whom.' This is a highly important evolution. Jesus proclaimed the kingdom of God; the early Christians proclaimed Jesus as king.

(V. 16)

Note the intimate address (cf. John 11–12), because the good shepherd knows his sheep by name (John 10:3). Mary turns *again* – physically or interiorly? It cannot be physical, because then she would have her back to Jesus. Instead, this turning is the interior conversion or journey of faith in the risen Lord.

(V. 17)

The Greek says literally 'do not keep touching me' (implied: treating me as you knew me before). It is peculiar that the resurrection is somehow incomplete because of the 'lifting up' theme in this gospel. Cf. 'I go to prepare a place'. The ascension underlines a break with Jesus as they knew him, only to open up a new way of relation. The distinction between my God and your God is only apparent – it is the one God, the gift is through Jesus going to 'his' God. The Greek has 'gone up', *anabainō*, an important word in this gospel. See John 1:51 (with angels); 3:13; 6:62 (NB).

(V. 18)

Mary is still the first to proclaim. Evidently not all believed – cf. John 20:25 (contrasted with 1 Corinthians 9:1). Mary bears witness, unlike Peter ('ask those who heard me; they know what I said'). In this way, she becomes the apostle of the apostles.

## Pointers for prayer

a)  The disciples are in a state of shock after their traumatic loss. Jesus, the one in whom they had placed so much hope, has been murdered and buried. Then, before they have time to recover they get another shock. The body of Jesus is missing. Have you had experiences in which one tragedy or crisis follows quickly after another? What was that like for you? How did you cope? Who, or what, sustained you?

b)  Mary and Peter, and the other disciple, came and discovered that the tomb was empty. In this text no explanation is given. They are left in a state of bewilderment, 'for as yet they did not understand the scripture, that he must rise from the dead'. Have you been in situations, faced with events you cannot explain, possibly events that have dashed your hopes in another person, or in God? What has that been like for you?

c)  Yet in spite of the lack of explanation, the beloved disciple 'saw and believed'. Have there been times when others have done something that you could not understand, and which they could not explain at the time, and yet you believed that all was not as it seemed; times when you decided to trust in spite of the evidence? Have there been times when others have shown this kind of faith in you, when you were not able to offer satisfactory explanations, and all you could say was 'trust me'?

d) Have there been times in your relationship with God when you have felt that you were faced with an empty tomb, and still you believed? What have you learned about life, about love, from such experiences?

## Prayer

*God of undying life, by your mighty hand you raised up Jesus from the grave and appointed him judge of the living and the dead. Bestow upon those baptised into his death the power flowing from his resurrection, that we may proclaim near and far the pardon and peace you give us. Amen.*

## ☙ Second Reading ☙

**Col 3:1** So if you have been raised with Christ, seek the things that are above, where Christ is, seated at the right hand of God. [2] Set your minds on things that are above, not on things that are on earth, [3] for you have died, and your life is hidden with Christ in God. [4] When Christ who is your life is revealed, then you also will be revealed with him in glory.

### Initial observations

Whatever else we may have expected to be told on Easter Sunday, it is unlikely that we anticipated being informed that we have died! The old joke about the premature announcement of our death may come to mind.

### Kind of writing

Colossians is a letter, but shading over into the 'epistolary sermon' typical of early Christianity. It is in three large segments, readily identifiable:

| | |
|---|---|
| 1:1–14 | Introduction |
| 1:15–4:6 | Body of the Letter |
| 4:7–18 | Conclusion |

Within the body of the letter, a new section starts at Colossians 3:1:

| | |
|---|---|
| 3:1–4 | Summary |
| 3:5–17 | Contrasting old and new |
| 3:18–4:1 | The Christian household |
| 4:2–6 | Advice and prayer |

Vv. 1–4 are a kind of heading, the contents of which will be amplified in the following verses.

## Origin of the reading

On account of the absence of typically Pauline vocabulary and the presence of non-typical words, many scholars assess Colossians to be a document of second-generation Paulinism, written in the name of the great apostle. Such an assessment is supported by a different theology with a cosmic view of Christ and a strong sense of realised eschatology.

Part of the presenting issue can be described thus. It seems that there are problems of 'spirituality' in the church at Colossae, with an emphasis on visions, angels, rituals, dietary restrictions and ascetic practices (it may sound familiar to many today).

> *Therefore do not let anyone condemn you in matters of food and drink or of observing festivals, new moons, or sabbaths. These are only a shadow of what is to come, but the substance belongs to Christ. Do not let anyone disqualify you, insisting on self-abasement and worship of angels, dwelling on visions, puffed up without cause by a human way of thinking, and not holding fast to the head, from whom the whole body, nourished and held together by its ligaments and sinews, grows with a growth that is from God.* (Colossians 2:16–19)

Such deviations have led to a denigration of the person and role of Jesus (perhaps also familiar today). The author insists, on the contrary, on the centrality and sufficiency of Christ, *for in him the whole fullness of deity dwells bodily, and you have come to fullness in him, who is the head of every ruler and authority* (Colossians 2:9–10). In effect, the writer is saying: You have all you need in Christ and there is no need for esoteric private revelations (also needed today).

## Related passages

I want their hearts to be encouraged and united in love, so that they may have all the riches of assured understanding and have the knowledge of God's mystery, that is, Christ himself, in whom are hidden all the treasures of wisdom and knowledge. (Colossians 2:2–3)

As you therefore have received Christ Jesus the Lord, continue to live your lives in him, rooted and built up in him and established in the faith, just as you were taught, abounding in thanksgiving. (Colossians 2:6–7)

And when you were dead in trespasses and the uncircumcision of your flesh, God made you alive together with him (Colossians 2:13)

If with Christ you died to the elemental spirits of the universe, why do you live as if you still belonged to the world? (Colossians 2:20)

## Brief commentary

(V. 1)
The little word 'so' makes the link between the orthodoxy of ch. 2 and the orthopraxis of ch. 3. Thus, the practical exhortations start here. The degree of the Christian's incorporation into Christ is reflected in the citations from ch. 2 above. Christ at God's right hand is one way of speaking of the resurrection, based on Psalm 110:1 (frequent in the New Testament).

(V. 2)

The writer expands a little on setting your minds on the things that are above. The contrast is with the human concoction of 'devotions' evolved in the Colossian community, judged to be earthly. The risk of an other-worldly dualism is obviated by the focus on Jesus now and in the future.

(V. 3)

The corollary of 'being raised' is that you (must!) have died. Cf. Colossians 2:20 above. Again, the purpose is the relativisation of attachment to esoteric asceticism. Hidden here means more than it can't be seen; it means also that it lies in the hand of God and in the future of God. Thus history has an unseen purpose in God. Hidden may also be a response to attraction of elite mysteries. The realised eschatology of Colossians is wisely tempered by the 'not yet' of the gospel. Cf. ...*because of the hope laid up for you in heaven* (Colossians 1:5).

(V. 4)

Notice the tension between the tenses: Christ *is* our life and yet we *will* be revealed with him in glory. Here, the writer stands very close to genuinely Pauline teaching and writings. However, in the view of Colossians, the *parousia* will bring nothing new – it will simply make plain what is already real for Christian believers.

## Pointers for prayer

a) The attraction to visions, angels and asceticism has not gone away and may very well detract from the central place of Christ in the Christian life.

b) The Christian tradition has sometimes settled for an other-worldly dualism, with an unhealthy detachment from living the Gospel *now*. How have I coped with such traditions and tensions?

c) To be told you have died may seem alarming, especially on Easter Sunday morning! To adapt Hebrews, we do really enjoy now something of the indestructible life (Hebrews 7:16) of Jesus, raised from the dead.

## Prayer

*On this glorious day of resurrection, faithful God, we praise you for all you have done for us in Jesus. He is our life. In him we have died and we are raised. In him we place all our hope.*

*Help us to live these gifts in the present moment so that others may be drawn to the life of faith and know the joy and happiness you offer us today and every day. Through Christ our Lord. Amen.*

## 🌿 First Reading 🌿

**Acts 10:34** Then Peter began to speak to them: 'I truly understand that God shows no partiality, [35] *but in every nation anyone who fears him and does what is right is acceptable to him.* [36] *You know the message he sent to the people of Israel, preaching peace by Jesus Christ – he is Lord of all.* [37] That message spread throughout Judea, beginning in Galilee after the baptism that John announced: [38] how God anointed Jesus of Nazareth with the Holy Spirit and with power; how he went about doing good and healing all who were oppressed by the devil, for God was with him. [39] We are witnesses to all that he did both in Judea and in Jerusalem. They put him to death by hanging him on a tree; [40] but God raised him on the third day and allowed him to appear, [41] not to all the people but to us who were chosen by God as witnesses, and who ate and drank with him after he rose from the dead. [42] He commanded us to preach to the people and to testify that he is the one ordained by God as judge of the living and the dead. [43] All the prophets testify about him that everyone who believes in him receives forgiveness of sins through his name.'

## Initial observations

The Acts of the Apostles is offered as history. However, it is not quite history as we would imagine it today. The writer does indeed use sources and tells a story in sequence. However, the overall purpose is persuasion, that is, to bring people to a new understanding of the Gospel. In particular, there are three dimensions that influence the telling: the role of the Holy Spirit, the ideals of the community and the career of Paul. Within that, the writer offers speeches at significant moments. How much of these go back to the events is a moot point. They seem to reflect a mature biblical appropriation of the Jesus tradition and reflect more or less entirely the language and outlook of the writer. Such 'history', with words put on the lips of characters, was completely normal at the time. The long story of Cornelius and his household occupies a pivotal position in the overall narrative and project of Luke–Acts. The biblical essay at the end of this volume may be of use.

## Kind of writing

This is a highly dramatic telling, unfolding in the context in a number of scenes and interludes:

|  |  |  |
|---|---|---|
|  | (9:43) | Peter a guest at home of Simon |
| *Scene 1* | (10:1–8) | Cornelius (revelation) |
| *Scene 2* | (10:9–16) | Peter (revelation) |
| *Scene 3* | (10:17–23a) | Peter meets the envoys of Cornelius |
| *Interlude* | (10:23b–27) | Journey of Peter and entourage; meeting of Peter and Cornelius |
| *Scene 4* | (10:28–48) | Peter and Cornelius in the latter's home in Caesarea |
| *Scene 5* | (11:1–18) | Peter explains his actions to the community at Jerusalem |

By means of this layout, Luke narrates the story of Cornelius no fewer than three times, without boring the hearers/readers. Our selection – vv. 34–43 – make up a distinct unit as follows:

*Scene 4b* (10:34–43)

| | | |
|---|---|---|
| A | vv. 34b–35 | Universalism |
| B | vv. 36–38 | Jesus – what he did |
| C | v. 39a | Witnesses |
| B* | vv. 39b–40 | Jesus – what was done to him |
| C* | vv. 41–42 | Witnesses |
| A* | v. 43 | Universalism |

## Origin of the reading

Acts 9:32–11:18 is a unit of teaching. There are three stories about Peter: (1) 9:32–35; (2) 9:36–43; (3) 10:1–11:18, which divides into (a) 10:1–19 the events and (b) 11:1–18 the justification of the events.

All three stories take place in Judea (incl. the administrative capital, Caesarea Maritima). The final report in Acts 11 is located in Jerusalem.

## Related Passages

'Fellow Israelites, I may say to you confidently of our ancestor David that he both died and was buried, and his tomb is with us to this day. Since he was a prophet, he knew that God had sworn with an oath to him that he would put one of his descendants on his throne. Foreseeing this, David spoke of the resurrection of the Messiah, saying, "He was not abandoned to Hades, nor did his flesh experience corruption." This Jesus God raised up, and of that all of us are witnesses. Being therefore exalted at the right hand of God, and having received from the Father the promise of the Holy Spirit, he has poured out this that you both see and hear. For David did not ascend into the heavens, but he himself says, "The Lord said to my Lord, 'Sit at my right hand, until I make your enemies your footstool.'" Therefore let the entire house of Israel know with certainty that God has made him both Lord and Messiah, this Jesus whom you crucified.' (Acts 2:29–36)

## Brief commentary

(Vv. 34b–35)

For lack of partiality: cf. Romans 2:11; Galatians 2:6; Colossians 3:25; Ephesians 6:9; 1 Peter 1:17; James 2:1, 9; *Testament of Job* 4:8; 1 *Clement* 1:3; *Barnabas* 4:12; Polycarp, *To the Philippians* 6:1b.

Some of these texts are not readily accessible, so here they are:

> And I will return you again to your goods. It will be repaid to you doubly, so you may know that the Lord is *impartial* – rendering good things to each one who obeys. (*Testament of Job* 4:7–8)

> For you did everything *without partiality*, and you lived in accordance with the laws of God, submitting yourselves to your leaders and giving to the older men among you the honour due them. (1 *Clement* 1:3)

> The Lord will judge the world *without partiality*. All will receive according to what they have done: if they are good, their righteousness will precede them; if they are evil, the wages of doing evil will go before them. (*Barnabas* 4:12)

> They must avoid all anger, *partiality*, unjust judgement, staying far away from all love of money; they must be neither quick to believe things spoken against anyone nor harsh in judgement, knowing that we are all in debt with respect to sin. (*To the Philippians* 6:1b)

(Vv. 36–38)

Jesus' activity as prophet is narrated, closely following the portrait in Luke's Gospel.

(V. 39a)

These are the witnesses to the ministry of Jesus. Being witnesses is central to the mission in the Acts of the Apostles.

(V. 39b–40)

Jesus is rejected (using the language of Galatians, interestingly); the resurrection (i.e. vindication) is the deed of God.

(Vv. 41–42)

These, again, are the witnesses to the resurrection of Jesus. Cf. Luke 24:36–43 (above); Acts 1:4.

(V. 43)

Universalism once more, as already implied in the Pentecost speech. Cf. *Peter said to them, 'Repent, and each one of you be baptised in the name of Jesus Christ for the forgiveness of your sins, and you will receive the gift of the Holy Spirit. For the promise is for you and your children, and for all who are far away, as many as the Lord our God will call to himself.'* (Acts 2:38–39) Cf. Luke 2:29–32; 3:6; 4:25–27; 24:47; Acts 1:8.

## Pointers for prayer

a) Witnesses: Who has been to me an authentic witness and bearer of the Good News? To whom have I been a witness?

b) Showing partiality is a very human trait and it takes conscious choice to act differently. How have I learned to accept people without prejudice?

c) The need for forgiveness is also a regular human phenomenon, sometimes from myself or from others; from time to time we need forgiveness also from God.

## Prayer

*God, creator of everything and everyone, lover of all humanity without partiality or distinction, help us to live according to the Good News of Jesus.*

*Help us to break down barriers just as he did. Show us how to reach out to the excluded, in imitation of Christ who was himself excluded in his execution, your Son, our Lord Jesus Christ, who lives and reigns with you in the unity of the Holy Spirit, God for ever and ever. Amen.*

## Themes across the readings

The gospel proclaims the resurrection, in Johannine mode, as an expression of love calling for a loving faith and a faithful love. Our second reading explores how we are to live our participation in the events of salvation. The first reading from the Acts serves to underline the universal offer of grace to all without distinction. Psalm 118 is perfect for the joyful, exultant thanksgiving for the reversal of the cross. Alleluia!

# Chapter 2

## Easter 2C

## Thought for the day

How did any of us make the journey towards faith in Christ? No doubt a great part of it is simply what we received – usually from family. At some point, did I make a conscious choice? At other times perhaps I felt like walking away from the faith project. What kept me going? Did a more personal ownership of faith result? Perhaps I have felt the intuition of John O'Donohue: 'Faith is helpless attraction to the divine.' In spite of everything, perhaps in spite of myself, somehow it is part of who I am.

## Prayer

*Mysterious God, we are those who have seen and at the same time not seen. Help to look beyond the simple gifts of each day to see you the giver behind – and in – every gift. Help us embrace the grace that we may know true blessedness in believing. Through Christ our risen Lord. Amen.*

## Gospel

**Jn 20:19** When it was evening on that day, the first day of the week, and the doors of the house where the disciples had met were locked for fear of the Jews, Jesus came and stood among them and said, 'Peace be with you.' [20] After he said this, he showed them his hands and his side. Then the disciples rejoiced when they saw the Lord. [21] Jesus said to them again, 'Peace be with you. As the Father has sent me, so I send you.' [22] When he had said this, he breathed on them and said to them, 'Receive the Holy Spirit. [23] If you forgive the sins of any, they are forgiven them; if you retain the sins of any, they are retained.'

[24] But Thomas (who was called the Twin), one of the twelve, was not with them when Jesus came. [25] So the other disciples told him, 'We have seen the Lord.' But he said to them, 'Unless I see the mark of the nails in his hands, and put my finger in the mark of the nails and my hand in his side, I will not believe.'

[26] A week later his disciples were again in the house, and Thomas was with them. Although the doors were shut, Jesus came and stood among them and said, 'Peace be with you.' [27] Then he said to Thomas, 'Put your finger here and see my hands. Reach out your hand and put it in my side. Do not doubt but believe.' [28] Thomas answered him, 'My Lord and my God!' [29] Jesus said to him, 'Have you believed because you have seen me? Blessed are those who have not seen and yet have come to believe.' [30] Now Jesus did many other signs in the presence of his disciples, which are not written in this book. [31] But these are written so that you may come to believe that Jesus is the Messiah, the Son of God, and that through believing you may have life in his name.

## Initial observations

Today we hear one of the most widely remembered stories from the New Testament: the story of doubting Thomas. It is interesting that that title has stuck, even though the point of the story is that Thomas actually arrives at faith. Perhaps we can identify more with the early stages …

Whereas the empty tomb proclamation narratives resemble each other in all four gospels, the resurrection appearance narratives are particular to each gospel. Even within that, the Fourth Gospel is always a bit special. For example, in the empty tomb proclamation narrative, it has significant features unique to itself – Mary Magdalene comes alone and there is the race between Peter and the Beloved Disciple and so on. The appearances of the Risen Lord are also peculiar to this gospel. In this excerpt, we hear the substantial story of Thomas, in two parts, followed by the first conclusion of the gospel. (Scholars often hold that ch. 21, while not original, was added very early, providing a secondary ending.)

## Kind of writing

This symbolic narrative explores several dimensions of Easter faith: (1) the gifts of the Risen Lord – peace, joy, the Spirit and forgiveness; (2) the identity of the Risen One with the Crucified One; (3) the blessedness of all who believe, eliminating any distinction between present believers and the very first generation of Christians. All three are important. Later generations may have felt that earlier Christians, who actually encountered the Risen Lord, were somehow more fortunate. Even more important, a later Christian heresy, Docetism – which denied the reality of Jesus' humanity and its continued significance after the resurrection – is countered by the sheer materiality of the Risen Lord.

## Old Testament background

> Then the Lord God formed man from the dust of the ground, and *breathed* into his nostrils the breath of life; and the man became a living being. (Genesis 2:7)

> … they failed to know the one who formed them and inspired them with active souls and breathed a living spirit into them. (Wisdom 15:11)

> Wake up! Bestir yourself for my defence, for my cause, my God and my Lord! (Psalm 35:23)

## New Testament foreground

(i) New creation in Christ is reflected in the layout of this gospel, which starts with an echo of Genesis 1:1. Jesus' last words on the cross are an echo of Genesis 2:2. John 20:1 explicitly recalls Genesis 1:1 again, and Genesis 2:7 is echoed in the breathing.

(ii) Holy Spirit/Advocate: In the Fourth Gospel, there is a wonderful and deep presentation of the Holy Spirit, the Advocate. A single verse gives an idea of what is at stake: *'Now he said this about the Spirit, which believers in him were to receive; for as yet there was no Spirit, because Jesus was not yet glorified'* (John 7:39). It is simply not the case that 'as yet there was no Spirit'! Yet the function of the Holy Spirit, in the light of the Paschal Mystery, is now so new, so different, that it is as if there had been no Spirit before. Cf. John 14:26; 16:7.

(iii) Peace: See John 14:27 and 16:33.

## St Paul

But how are they to call on one in whom they have not believed? And how are they to believe in one of whom they have never heard? And how are they to hear without someone to proclaim him? And how are they to proclaim him unless they are sent? As it is written, 'How beautiful are the feet of those who bring good news!' But not all have obeyed the good news; for Isaiah says, 'Lord, who has believed our message?' So faith comes from what is heard, and what is heard comes through the word of Christ. (Romans 10:14–17)

## Brief commentary

(V. 19)
That is, the day of creation. Jesus' self-presentation is not impeded in any way by their fear. Peace here is the Easter good news of victory over death and even over the fear of death.

(V. 20)

That is, the Risen One is the Crucified and the Crucified is the Risen One. Jesus is both the same and utterly transformed. The first gift was peace, the second gift is joy.

(V. 21)

Repetition for emphasis. 'As' should read 'just as' and means more than a formal similarity: Jesus' very own mission from the Father continues unbroken in the mission of the disciples.

(V. 22)

Here we have the echoes of the first creation story. The third gift (after peace and the mission) is the Holy Spirit, in the new role of Advocate and rememberer. A new creation in Christ is a strong early Christian experience and proclamation. 'For neither circumcision nor uncircumcision is anything; but a *new creation* is everything!' (Galatians 6:15). 'So if anyone is in Christ, there is a *new creation*: everything old has passed away; see, everything has become new!' (2 Corinthians 5:17). 'Blessed be the God and Father of our Lord Jesus Christ! By his great mercy he has given us a *new birth* into a living hope through the resurrection of Jesus Christ from the dead' (1 Peter 1:3).

(V. 23)

The fourth gift – to all believers – is forgiveness of sins. In this episode, forgiveness is part of the mission of the whole church. (It seems here are no ministerial offices in the Johannine communities.) 'Holding on' to sins means blocking God's grace by withholding the gift of forgiveness.

(V. 24)

Thomas was profiled earlier in the gospel: John 11:16; 14:5.

(V. 25)

Believe what? That he is risen? That it is the same Jesus? That he is simply alive again?

(V. 26)

The careful timing indicates the eighth day, that is, today, one week after Easter Sunday. The very same gift of peace is given again. This is no mere greeting. Instead, the risen Lord offers the peace of freedom from the power and fear of death itself.

(V. 27)

The Risen Lord now takes the initiative, by meeting the heartfelt questions and doubts of Thomas. It is not clear how Jesus mysteriously knows what had happened previously.

(V. 28)

This is the highest proclamation of Jesus' identity in this gospel. In this way, deepest doubt can be the direct road to exalted faith. The words also counter the propaganda of the Roman emperors, one of whom, Domitian, preferred to be addressed as 'our lord and our God' (*Dominus et deus noster*), no less.

(V. 29)

This is a beatitude, one of the twenty-seven New Testament beatitudes. The writer is most likely meeting an anxiety at the time of writing when the third and fourth generations of Christians may have felt that the difference in time from the events of salvation put them at something of a disadvantage. In no way!

(V. 30)

This is the first ending of the gospel and is a frank admission that the writer has selected from many traditions. The second ending, in ch. 21, is in the same vein: *But there are also many other things that Jesus did; if every one of them were written down, I suppose that the world itself could not contain the books that would be written* (John 21:25).

(V. 31)

This is a key text for understanding the nature of the gospels and in particular the kind of text that the Fourth Gospel is. The goal is a true understanding of the identity of the risen Jesus so that believers may believe in him and from him draw life.

## Pointers for prayer

a) 'Peace be with you' was the greeting of Jesus on meeting his frightened apostles. Who has come to you bringing peace at times when you were afraid? To whom have you been able to bring peace?

b) Thomas, doubting and questioning, is possibly a person with whom we can identify. What part have doubting and questioning played on your faith journey? How has your faith been strengthened by such moments?

c) Note the way that Jesus dealt with Thomas. He did not take him to task because he doubted. He accepted how he felt and led him along to see the truth of his resurrection. Who has been that kind of teacher for you, gently taking you where you were and leading you to a deeper knowledge about some truth about life? For whom have you been that kind of teacher?

d) 'Blessed are they who have not seen and yet believed.' That requires great trust. Perhaps you have had the experience of being trusted without having to justify every step along the way. What was it like to be trusted in that way? Whom have you been able to trust in a similar manner?

## Prayer

*God of life, source of all faith, through the waters of baptism you have raised us up in Christ and given us life that endures.*

*Day by day, refine our faith that we, who have not seen the Christ, may truly confess him as our Lord and God, and share the blessedness of those who believe.*

*Grant this through Jesus Christ, the resurrection and the life, who lives and reigns with you in the unity of the Holy Spirit, God for ever and ever. Amen.*

## 🌿 Second Reading 🌿

**Rev 1:9** I, John, your brother who shares with you in Jesus the persecution and the kingdom and the patient endurance, was on the island called Patmos because of the word of God and the testimony of Jesus. ¹⁰ I was in the spirit on the Lord's day, and I heard behind me a loud voice like a trumpet ¹¹ saying, 'Write in a book what you see and send it to the seven churches, to Ephesus, to Smyrna, to Pergamum, to Thyatira, to Sardis, to Philadelphia, and to Laodicea.'

¹² Then I turned to see whose voice it was that spoke to me, and on turning I saw seven golden lamp stands, ¹³ and in the midst of the lamp stands I saw one like the Son of Man, clothed with a long robe and with a golden sash across his chest. ¹⁴ *His head and his hair were white as white wool, white as snow; his eyes were like a flame of fire,* ¹⁵ *his feet were like burnished bronze, refined as in a furnace, and his voice was like the sound of many waters.* ¹⁶ *In his right hand he held seven stars, and from his mouth came a sharp, two-edged sword, and his face was like the sun shining with full force.*

¹⁷ When I saw him, I fell at his feet as though dead. But he placed his right hand on me, saying, 'Do not be afraid; I am the first and the last, ¹⁸ and the living one. I was dead, and see, I am alive for ever and ever; and I have the keys of Death and of Hades. ¹⁹ Now write what you have seen, what is, and what is to take place after this.'

## Initial observations

For Eastertide in Year C the lectionary offers us a judicious selection of readings from the New Testament Apocalypse. This book is not otherwise read on Sundays except for Christ the King in Year B. Everyone recognises that the book of Revelation is not easy to read and that it presents a challenge for the ordinary listener. A little perseverance will pay dividends, however.

The book of Revelation speaks to a constant concern: how to square belief in God with the fact of evil and suffering. As such it corresponds in the New Testament to the book of Job in the Old Testament. As part of its response, it offers the highest Christology of the New Testament, combined with a thoroughgoing theology of incarnation and suffering. In a word, God now 'rules' through vulnerability, because in Jesus God has entered the human story, especially in its darkness and tragedy. See Revelation 5:6.

## Kind of writing

Apocalyptic refers to a spiritual movement (see above in relation to theodicy) and a kind of writing. Our New Testament Apocalypse is an example of a vision apocalypse. Using a potent combination of biblical, political, mythological and liturgical allusions, the book takes seriously the hardship undergone by believers while reassuring them that in Christ victory is already assured. He even offers a (somewhat premature) mock funeral liturgy for the empire, by way of concrete illustration.

## Origin of the reading

The setting is Asia Minor (western Turkey today), as we see from the named cities. The context is twofold: (i) some kind of severe oppression, if not quite persecution, on account of the faith; and (ii) emperor worship. The latter is widespread, even 'in your face', and participation was regarded as a test of loyalty to the state. In general, the book of Revelation is quite damning about the Roman Empire – in its view, the latest and worst 'incarnation' of evil empires from time immemorial.

## Related Passages

> The revelation of Jesus Christ, which God gave him to show his servants what must soon take place; he made it known by sending his angel to his servant John, who testified to the

word of God and to the testimony of Jesus Christ, even to all that he saw. Blessed is the one who reads aloud the words of the prophecy, and blessed are those who hear and who keep what is written in it; for the time is near. (Revelation 1:1–3)

'See, I am coming soon; my reward is with me, to repay according to everyone's work. I am the Alpha and the Omega, the first and the last, the beginning and the end.' (Revelation 22:12–13)

## Brief commentary

(V. 9)
The writer closes the gap with the readers: he shares the persecution and he too is called to perseverance and to testimony. Because of the shared experience, he can speak to them directly.

(V. 10)
We are meant to think of an ecstatic and overwhelming experience, later digested and presented with immense literary skill as our Revelation.

(V. 11)
These cities were carefully chosen to represent the typical challenges of the time – including emperor worship and simply losing fervour, even faith itself.

(V. 12)
The seven golden lamp stands evoke the decoration of the Temple and thus represent the presence of God. As the vision unfolds, we learn that the lamp stands also represent the seven communities named.

(V. 13)
The imagery is taken from Daniel 7:13.

(Vv. 14–16)
These verses are intense, evocative and mysterious ... and, of course, anything but literal. Their omission in the lectionary makes the reaction of dread collapse in v. 17 more difficult to grasp. In any case, the seer

presents his vision as extraordinary and overwhelming, with a great deal of allusion to the Old Testament. Notes in your study bible will be of help here.

(V. 17a)
Such collapse is the correct etiquette should one ever receive such a vision (Ezekiel 1:28; Daniel 9:18).

(Vv. 17b–18)
The language is taken from the Old Testament (see Isaiah 44:6) and will resonate throughout the Apocalypse. Cf. Revelation 1:8; 2:8; 21:6; 22:12–13 (above). The resurrection is proclaimed, followed by Jesus' power over death, symbolised by the keys. Cf: Revelation 3:7; 9:1; 20:1.

(V. 19)
NB: *Blessed is the one who reads aloud the words of the prophecy, and blessed are those who hear and who keep what is written in it; for the time is near* (Revelation 1:3; also 22:18–19!).

## Pointers for prayer

a) Go back in your own mind to some time when you had an intense experience of 'presence,' an awareness of God-with-you. This may help you enter this reading.

b) More or less everyone in the Bible is told at some point not to be afraid. It is part of the deep reassurance of faith, a reassurance we need and should not be afraid to acknowledge.

## Prayer

*God, giver of all life, source of resurrection hope, lead us to a deep faith in Jesus, risen from the dead, and give us courage to live our faith fully, from the inside out. Through Christ our Lord. Amen.*

## 🌿 First Reading 🌿

**Acts 5:12** Now many signs and wonders were done among the people through the apostles. And they were all together in Solomon's Portico. [13] None of the rest dared to join them, but the people held them in high esteem. [14] Yet more than ever believers were added to the Lord, great numbers of both men and women, [15] so that they even carried out the sick into the streets, and laid them on cots and mats, in order that Peter's shadow might fall on some of them as he came by. [16] A great number of people would also gather from the towns around Jerusalem, bringing the sick and those tormented by unclean spirits, and they were all cured.

## Initial observations

The passage chosen is a summary passage found frequently in the Acts. The immediately preceding context is important to appreciate the significance of this summary.

The Acts of the Apostles purports to be history; it is not, however, so straightforward or simple. Three different kinds of 'history' overlap in this marvellous writing:

Documentary History
*Chiefly raw facts, dates, documents and data. Examples in Acts: geography, politics, Roman institutions, place names etc.*

Explanatory History
*An attempt at explanation, drawing to gather context, personalities, causes and consequences, usually in some narrative sequence.*

Poetic History
*An attempt to speak to the present moment, by means of a selective retelling of the past. In this case, the desire to instruct and uplift is paramount. Examples in Acts: the first Pentecost, the conversion of Cornelius, the shipwreck of St Paul.*

In a word, the book of Acts is not a novel, nor biography, nor history, nor apologetics in any strict sense, through it has features of all these genres. Rather, it is best viewed as a narrative of origins, broadly historical and strongly apologetic, aimed at instructing the hearers/readers at the time of writing.

*Context within Acts*

In Acts 4:24–5:42, we hear of increasing hostility towards the Way. In contrast, there is a counter theme, the inexorable expansion of the church.

## Kind of writing

The summary is laid out in chiastic fashion, as follows:

| A  | vv. 12–13a | answer to the petitions in 4:29–30 |
|----|------------|------------------------------------|
| B  | v. 13b     | response of people to the apostles |
| B* | v. 14      | response of people to the apostles |
| A* | vv. 15–16  | answer to the petition in 4:30     |

See Acts 4:24–30 below for the background.

## Origin of the reading

Acts was most likely penned in the early second century, in Rome. It may resonate with Jewish revolts in the Diaspora (AD 115–117). The pastoral content feels like that of the late Pastorals: 'wolves', heresy, rejection of the Old Testament, unease with the empire, yet no direct persecution. The warm affirmation of the Jewish roots of Christianity may be a response to what later emerged under Marcion, who promoted a wholesale rejection of the mother religion.

## Related passages

> When they heard it, they raised their voices together to God and said, 'Sovereign Lord, who made the heaven and the earth, the sea, and everything in them, it is you who said by the Holy Spirit through our ancestor David, your servant:

'Why did the Gentiles rage, and the peoples imagine vain things? The kings of the earth took their stand, and the rulers have gathered together against the Lord and against his Messiah.' For in this city, in fact, both Herod and Pontius Pilate, with the Gentiles and the peoples of Israel, gathered together against your holy servant Jesus, whom you anointed, to do whatever your hand and your plan had predestined to take place. And now, Lord, look at their threats, and grant to your servants to speak your word with all boldness, while you stretch out your hand to heal, and signs and wonders are performed through the name of your holy servant Jesus.' (Acts 4:24–30)

Cf. summaries in Acts 2:42–47 and 4:32–37.

## Brief commentary

(V. 12)
The summary picks up the miraculous in the preceding episode (Acts 5:12; see 2:43 and 4:30), done through the hands of the apostles (see also Acts 14:3; 19:19; cf. 8:17; 9:41: 11:30).

Solomon's portico is mentioned in Acts 3:11 and John 10:23. It was a covered walkway formed by rows of columns supporting a roof and open on the inner side facing the centre of the temple complex. Located beside the Court of the Gentiles, it was a very public area.

(V. 13)
'None of the rest' seems to be an exaggeration in the light of v. 14, when some did join them. Nevertheless, the group is beginning to have a distinct identity. The people's reaction is a recognition of the divine at work: Acts 10:46; 19:17; Luke 1:46, 58 and many psalms.

(V. 14)
The messianic community is identified as 'the believers' (cf. 2:44; 5:32). The increase is regularly noted (cf. 2:41; 4:4). The NRSV has 'added to the Lord', but 'added by the Lord' is better.

(V. 15)

These are examples of the signs and wonders. Notice that Peter is the focus of attention. Cf. the healing power of Jesus' clothing in Luke 8:44 and the cloths touched by Paul (Acts 19:12). Women are specifically mentioned for the first time as a group.

(V. 16)

This verse takes us out of the Temple and even out of Jerusalem. A considerable expansion is implied.

## Pointers for prayer

a) Hostility to the faith (or at least to the Church) is not unknown in our day. Perhaps we too are called to show courage and to speak the word with all boldness?

b) The scene is one of healing and recognition of need. What needs do I bring before the Lord for his healing touch?

c) The women are clearly important for Luke (cf. 'some women of our group astounded us'). How do I see the evolution of the role of women in the Church?

## Prayer

*God of salvation, you offer life to all through Jesus and the preaching of the Word. Show us how to bring that word of life and healing to the people of our time. Through Christ our Lord. Amen.*

## Themes across the readings

These readings present two contrasting moments: crowds joining the Way and an individual struggling with faith. The image of rapid expansion may encourage but the journey is always individual. The verses from Psalm 118 (117) are a generic thanksgiving. However, one verse was used by early Christians to speak of the death and resurrection of Jesus: The stone which the builders rejected has become the cornerstone.

# Chapter 3

## Easter 3C

### Thought for the day

In our ordinary world, words such as compassion, forgiveness and reconciliation convey an essential, if difficult, and at the same time joyful, human task. In our world of faith, we add other words, such as mercy and grace, which make us conscious of the free gift, unalloyed, with no conditions attached. Our role is not to 'retain the sins of any', precisely so that they may know, at our hands, true forgiveness. In our gospel, Peter is not reproached; rather he is set free. That is love, the only commandment.

### Prayer

*Lord Jesus, help us all to hear your invitation, 'Do you love me?'*
*and set our hearts free to practise forgiveness in your name.*
*You live and reign for ever and ever. Amen.*

### 🌿 Gospel 🌿

**Jn 21:1** After these things Jesus showed himself again to the disciples by the Sea of Tiberias; and he showed himself in this way. ² Gathered there together were Simon Peter, Thomas called the Twin, Nathanael of Cana in Galilee, the sons of Zebedee, and two others of his disciples. ³ Simon Peter said to them, 'I am going fishing.' They said to him, 'We will go with you.' They went out and got into the boat, but that night they caught nothing. ⁴ Just after daybreak, Jesus stood on the beach; but the disciples did not know that it was Jesus. ⁵ Jesus said to them, 'Children, you have no fish, have you?' They answered him, 'No.' ⁶ He said to them, 'Cast the net to the right side of the boat, and you will find some.' So they cast it, and now they were not able to haul it in because there were so many fish. ⁷ That disciple whom Jesus loved said to Peter, 'It is the Lord!' When Simon Peter heard that it was the Lord, he put on some clothes, for he was naked, and jumped into the sea. ⁸ But the other disciples came in the boat, dragging the net full of fish, for they were not far from the land, only about a hundred yards off. ⁹ When they had gone ashore, they saw a charcoal fire there, with fish on it, and bread. ¹⁰ Jesus said to them, 'Bring some of the fish that you have just caught.' ¹¹ So Simon Peter went aboard and hauled the net ashore, full of large fish, a hundred fifty-three of them; and though there were so many, the net was not torn. ¹² Jesus said to them, 'Come and have breakfast.' Now none of the disciples dared to ask him, 'Who are you?' because they knew it was the Lord. ¹³ Jesus came and took the bread and gave it to them, and did the same with the fish. ¹⁴ This was now the third time that Jesus appeared to the disciples after he was raised from the dead.

¹⁵ When they had finished breakfast, Jesus said to Simon Peter, 'Simon son of John, do you love me more than these?' He said to him, 'Yes, Lord; you know that I love you.' Jesus said to him, 'Feed my lambs.' ¹⁶ A second time he said to him, 'Simon son of John, do you love me?' He said to him, 'Yes, Lord; you know that I love you.' Jesus said to him, 'Tend my sheep.' ¹⁷ He said to him the third time, 'Simon son of John, do you love me?' Peter felt hurt because he said to him the third time, 'Do you love me?' And he said to him, 'Lord, you know everything; you know that I love you.' Jesus said to him, 'Feed my sheep. ¹⁸ Very truly, I tell you, when you were younger, you used to fasten your own belt and to go wherever

you wished. But when you grow old, you will stretch out your hands, and someone else will fasten a belt around you and take you where you do not wish to go.' [19] (He said this to indicate the kind of death by which he would glorify God.) After this, he said to him, 'Follow me.'

## Initial observations

There are two scenes here, with the first scene laying the ground for the second one. For the ordinary reader, these stories come as a surprise after the apparent conclusion in John 20:30–31. Why the addition? It seems to have been written after the 'death' of the major figure of this gospel:

> Jesus said to him, 'If it is my will that he remain until I come, what is that to you? Follow me!' So the rumour spread in the community that this disciple would not die. Yet Jesus did not say to him that he would not die, but, 'If it is my will that he remain until I come, what is that to you?' (John 21:22–23)

Until that moment, this Johannine community seems to have got along without a leadership structure and without a link to the 'great' church, symbolised by Peter. The whole text functions as a kind of accord, whereby the Johannine community comes to recognise the role of Peter, through a reminder of his fundamental call and through his threefold rehabilitation, significantly around a charcoal fire. Resurrection appearance narratives are highly symbolic in nature, usually reflecting critical issues at the time of writing.

## Kind of writing

These scenes belong to a familiar pattern found in the resurrection appearance narratives in Matthew, Luke and John: the initiative of Jesus, non-recognition, recognition and then mission. However, the first story closely resembles an expanded call story in Luke 5 (see below).

## Old Testament background

I myself will be the shepherd of my sheep, and I will make them lie down, says the Lord God. I will seek the lost, and I will bring back the strayed, and I will bind up the injured, and I will strengthen the weak, but the fat and the strong I will destroy. I will feed them with justice. ... I will set up over them one shepherd, my servant David, and he shall feed them: he shall feed them and be their shepherd. And I, the Lord, will be their God, and my servant David shall be prince among them; I, the Lord, have spoken. (Ezekiel 34:15–16, 23–24)

## New Testament foreground

(i)  This text has some kind of link with a similar passage found in Luke 5:1–11, an expanded call story in that context.

Once while Jesus was standing beside the lake of Gennesaret, and the crowd was pressing in on him to hear the word of God, he saw two boats there at the shore of the lake; the fishermen had gone out of them and were washing their nets. He got into one of the boats, the one belonging to Simon, and asked him to put out a little way from the shore. Then he sat down and taught the crowds from the boat. When he had finished speaking, he said to Simon, 'Put out into the deep water and let down your nets for a catch.' Simon answered, 'Master, we have worked all night long but have caught nothing. Yet if you say so, I will let down the nets.' When they had done this, they caught so many fish that their nets were beginning to break. So they signalled their partners in the other boat to come and help them. And they came and filled both boats, so that they began to sink. But when Simon Peter saw it, he fell down at Jesus' knees, saying, 'Go away from me, Lord, for I am a sinful man!' For he and all who were with him were amazed at the catch of fish that they had taken; and so also were James and John, sons of Zebedee, who were partners with Simon. Then Jesus said to Simon, 'Do not be afraid; from now on you will be catching people.' When they had brought their boats to shore, they left everything and followed him. (Luke 5:1–11)

*Shared aspects*

- Fishing all night and catching nothing
- Jesus' command to cast the net
- The extraordinary catch
- The risk to the net
- The reaction of Simon Peter
- Jesus is called 'Lord'
- The other fishermen help but are silent
- The symbolism pointing to the mission
- Shared vocabulary to do with fishing, such as getting on board, landing, net and so forth

*Unique aspects*

- In John, Jesus is not at first recognised
- In John, Jesus stands on the shore
- In John, you have the Beloved Disciple and Simon Peter
- In John, others haul in the fish
- In John, the net is not torn but in Luke it is breaking
- In John, the catch is close to the shore and dragged to it
- In John, Peter rushes to the Lord; in Luke, he begs Jesus to go away from him

Here we have a single gospel tradition, which has arrived independently in each gospel.

(ii)   There is also some kind of link with the establishment of the authority of Peter in the New Testament. Matthew alone has this passage, after the confession of Peter at Caesarea Philippi:

And Jesus answered him, 'Blessed are you, Simon son of Jonah! For flesh and blood has not revealed this to you, but my Father in heaven. And I tell you, you are Peter, and on this rock I will build my church, and the gates of Hades will not prevail against it. I will give you the keys of the kingdom of heaven, and whatever you bind on earth will be bound in heaven, and whatever you loose on earth will be loosed in heaven.' Then he sternly ordered the disciples not to tell anyone that he was the Messiah. (Matthew 16:16–20)

(iii) 'To draw' has a special usage in John's Gospel: No one can come to me unless drawn by the Father who sent me; and I will raise that person up on the last day (John 6:44). And I, when I am lifted up from the earth, will draw all people to myself (John 12:32).

## St Paul

While we were staying there for several days, a prophet named Agabus came down from Judea. He came to us and took Paul's belt, bound his own feet and hands with it, and said, 'Thus says the Holy Spirit, "This is the way the Jews in Jerusalem will bind the man who owns this belt and will hand him over to the Gentiles."' When we heard this, we and the people there urged him not to go up to Jerusalem. Then Paul answered, 'What are you doing, weeping and breaking my heart? For I am ready not only to be bound but even to die in Jerusalem for the name of the Lord Jesus.' Since he would not be persuaded, we remained silent except to say, 'The Lord's will be done.' (Acts 21:10–14)

## Brief commentary

(Vv. 1)
In the New Testament, this gospel is the only one to use the name Tiberias for the Sea of Galilee, so we are still within the Johannine tradition. The other links are also to do with the sea and with an epiphany (cf. John 6:1, 23).

(V. 2)
The list of names is highly unusual, because it expands the usual trio (Peter, James and John) to include characters with a noted role in this

gospel (Thomas and Nathanael, recalling the end and the beginning of Jesus' ministry), as well as two unnamed figures.

(V. 3)

This is a strange proposal, representing what? Hardly a desire to go back to his ordinary life. Rather, it is essential for the setting up of the story. 'Night' is always special in John: the time of evil, the time of separation: 'Night is coming when no one can work' (John 9:4). Perhaps it represents the disorientation of the Johannine community after the death of the Beloved Disciple, as well as the need to rediscover the fundamentals of the call of Jesus, as they faced a new beginning.

(V. 4)

Lack of recognition is part of these Easter stories. Suddenly it is morning, that is, on account of Jesus' presence, night is over.

(V. 5)

'Children' is the special address of the Johannine community to its members (see 1 John 2:14, 18, for the diminutive – little children – as here in John 21).

(V. 6)

Here we are very close to Luke 5.

(V. 7)

Peter still needs the prompting of the 'disciple whom Jesus loved'. The characteristic impetuosity of Peter was widely remembered, leaving its mark even in later symbolic scenes.

(V. 8)

The quick arrival resembles John 6:21.

(V. 9)

Charcoal is an explicit evocation of the fire in John 18:18, where the same unusual word is used. The word is *anthrakia*, from which our word anthracite.

(V. 10)

Meals were typical of the ministry of Jesus and are here evoked in a resurrection setting, as in the Emmaus story.

(V. 11)

Notice the prominence of Peter – he acts alone, although seven people are present. The number of fish has given rise to very interesting speculation. There is a late claim in Jerome that 153 was the known number of species of fish at the time. That would fit with the symbolism of the catch – the Petrine ministry is universal or 'catholic'.

(V. 12)

Jesus is now the real host of the gathering and issues the invitation.

(V. 13)

Here we have an explicit echo of John 6 and also of the Lord's Supper (even though that is not recounted in this gospel).

(V. 14)

The counting of the days 'stitches' this story into the preceding chapter. It is an explicit editorial comment or voice to make sure we know what the story is about.

(V. 15)

The threefold questioning is clearly an evocation of the threefold denial. The writer alternates the words for love (*agapaō* and *phileō*), but this variation seems to bear no special meaning. The full phrase 'son of John' is found only in John 1:42, but insisted upon here. In the earlier text, the name Cephas is given without any confession of faith, simply a future statement of greatness. Here, in ch. 21, that promise is fulfilled.

(V. 16)

Repetition is used, triggering rising tension in the reader and dismay in Peter.

(V. 17)

Eventually, Peter is affected and he reacts. An echo of John 16:20, where we read: 'Very truly, I tell you, you will weep and mourn, but the world will rejoice; you will have pain, but your pain will turn into joy' (John 16:20).

(V. 18)

This was written long after the death of Peter. Cf. John 15:8 and 12:26. The death of Peter is not recounted in the New Testament. The death, however, is noticed by several writers, such as Clement I, Tertullian and Eusebius of Caesarea. The source for the traditional story of his being crucified upside down is the Acts of Peter, 37.8: 'I request you therefore, executioners, to crucify me head-downwards – in this way and no other. And the reason I will tell to those who hear.'

(V. 19)

The very first, foundational call of Jesus in the gospels is explicitly evoked. Even in advanced resurrection scenes, the core of that call remains at the heart of ministry.

## Pointers for prayer

a) The disciples spend a fruitless night fishing and catching nothing. Things change dramatically when Jesus appears and invites them to try again. Remember those who came to you and encouraged you to try again when you felt discouraged. Perhaps on some of these occasions the results were beyond your expectations.

b) The story can serve as a reminder that sometimes we are wasting our time if we try to work on our own without the Lord's help. When have you found that your work or life was more fruitful when you acknowledged that you needed God's help and you spoke to God about your need?

c) Peter is given the chance to be fully reconciled with his Master after his denial during the Passion. Remember those who have given you an opportunity for reconciliation after you had hurt them or let them down. What was it like for you to be given this chance? To whom have you offered the possibility of reconciliation?

## Prayer

*God of life, in your risen Son you reveal your abiding presence among us and summon those reborn in baptism to lives of worship and service. Fill this assembly with reverence as we come before you in prayer. Grant us courage and zeal in bearing witness before the world to your Son, Jesus Christ, the first-born from the dead, who lives and reigns with you in the unity of the Holy Spirit, God for ever and ever. Amen.*

## 🌿 Second Reading 🌿

**Rev 5:11** Then I looked, and I heard the voice of many angels surrounding the throne and the living creatures and the elders; they numbered myriads of myriads and thousands of thousands, [12] singing with full voice,

'Worthy is the Lamb that was slaughtered
to receive power and wealth and wisdom and might
and honour and glory and blessing!'
[13] Then I heard every creature in heaven and on earth and under the earth and in the sea, and all that is in them, singing,
'To the one seated on the throne and to the Lamb
be blessing and honour and glory and might
forever and ever!'
[14] And the four living creatures said, 'Amen!' And the elders fell down and worshipped.

### Initial observations

Our reading reminds us of the significance of the liturgy in the Apocalypse. Revelation has many liturgical elements, such as hymns, responses, places of worship, even liturgies, both mocking and in earnest. It is even likely that the whole book was meant to be performed in some way, a kind of enacted prophecy cum apocalypse, with lively participation in the hymns, taken from the repertoire of the community. In this way, the author encourages 'ownership' of the message through the texts already familiar from the liturgy.

With the renewed use of these hymns in the post-Second Vatican Council breviary, we may also have a sense of the reassuringly familiar. On Tuesdays, the New Testament canticle for Evening Prayer is taken precisely from Revelation 4:11; 5:9, 10, 12.

The power of the text is given thrilling voice in Handel's *Messiah*. He chose to close the entire drama of the Christ with this text in movement 53, a fitting act of worship and prayer.

## Kind of writing

After the opening vision and the letters to the seven churches, Revelation 4–5 forms the foundation for the rest of the Apocalypse. From ch. 6 onwards, the writer reflects back to the community their experience of suffering, especially at the hands of the empire. There is no understatement of evil in the Apocalypse – on the contrary! – and the portrait of destructive forces could be quite overwhelming. It is significant, therefore, that this grim parade is preceded by the immensely reassuring chs 4–5, guaranteeing future victory before the battle begins.

There are four sections to the vision: 4:1–11; 5:1–5, 6–10 and 11–14. This pattern, perhaps in some measure resembling synagogue worship and Christian liturgy, may help:

> I. 4:1–11: the *Kedushah*, on God's holiness in creation, as the foundation for his act of redemption.
> II. 5:1–5: the *Shema*, celebrating the gift of the Torah and the new Scroll, which only the Lamb can open.
> III. 5:6–10: *Gelulah* or redemption, recounting the cross and resurrection in the symbolic language of the Apocalypse.
> IV. 5:11–14: *Doxology*, bringing together the present earthly and future heavenly liturgies, from which the membership may draw strength.

## Origin of the reading

The community was undergoing some experience of societal alienation – especially in regard to emperor worship – and perhaps a level of harassment, if not quite persecution. The question arose, where to find strength to stay faithful? Our New Testament Apocalypse teaches that faith in the Lamb, still bearing the marks of one slain, is central. At the same time, the members encounter this risen Lord in the liturgy and the common prayer is meant to be the source of strength for the faithful.

## Related passages

The New Testament Apocalypse never cites the Bible, but almost every verse alludes to a biblical text of some kind. Here, for example, we may note:

> V. 11: Then Micaiah said, 'Therefore hear the word of the LORD: I saw the LORD sitting on his throne, with all the host of heaven standing beside him to the right and to the left of him (1 Kings 22:19). A stream of fire issued and flowed out from his presence. A thousand thousands served him, and ten thousand times ten thousand stood attending him. The court sat in judgment, and the books were opened (Daniel 7:10).

> V. 12: Yours, O LORD, are the greatness, the power, the glory, the victory, and the majesty; for all that is in the heavens and on the earth is yours; yours is the kingdom, O LORD, and you are exalted as head above all (1 Chronicles 29:11). He was oppressed, and he was afflicted, yet he did not open his mouth; like a lamb that is led to the slaughter, and like a sheep that before its shearers is silent, so he did not open his mouth (Isaiah 53:7). God is king over the nations; God sits on his holy throne (Psalm 47:8) who made heaven and earth, the sea, and all that is in them; who keeps faith forever (Psalm 146:6). In the year that King Uzziah died, I saw the LORD sitting on a throne, high and lofty; and the hem of his robe filled the temple (Isaiah 6:1). And above the dome over their heads there was something like a throne, in appearance

like sapphire; and seated above the likeness of a throne was something that seemed like a human form. Upward from what appeared like the loins I saw something like gleaming amber, something that looked like fire enclosed all around; and downward from what looked like the loins I saw something that looked like fire, and there was a splendour all around (Ezekiel 1:26–27). There is but one who is wise, greatly to be feared, seated upon his throne– the Lord (Sirach 1:8).

V. 13: Then Micaiah said, 'Therefore hear the word of the Lord: I saw the Lord sitting on his throne, with all the host of heaven standing to the right and to the left of him (2 Chronicles 18:18).

V. 14: Over the heads of the living creatures there was something like a dome, shining like crystal, spread out above their heads (Ezekiel 1:22). In the middle of it was something like four living creatures. This was their appearance: they were of human form (Ezekiel 1:5). Their entire body, their rims, their spokes, their wings, and the wheels – the wheels of the four of them – were full of eyes all around (Ezekiel 10:12). Each one had four faces: the first face was that of the cherub, the second face was that of a human being, the third that of a lion, and the fourth that of an eagle (Ezekiel 10:14).

For the intended hearers, this resonance with the Bible would have bestowed great authority to the newly minted text of the Apocalypse.

## Brief commentary

(V. 11)
Once the fulfilment of redemption has been achieved, there takes place a vast act of worship, which includes innumerable angels, the animals and the elders, who proclaim the sevenfold worthiness of the Lamb. His worthiness enables him to unlock the seven-sealed scroll.

(V. 12)

The hymn repeats what may be an element of early Christian liturgy, 'Worthy is the Lamb …'. The ascription is sevenfold, indicating perfection. The lamb is 'still bearing the marks of one slain.' In Greek, this is a perfect participle, which denotes that the effects have continued into the present time. The risen Jesus takes with him, even into his victory, the experience of suffering. At the same time, this is a kind of proleptic, anticipatory liturgy, looking forward to the final victory over evil.

(V. 13)

This act of worship is shared by all creation, very fully conjured up. This is all done before the Apocalypse describes woes etc. A reasonable case could be made for saying that the Apocalypse teaches the salvation of all humanity eventually. Then follows a fourfold blessing, appropriately following the fourfold sketch of creation.

(V. 14)

Finally, the worship on earth is echoed in heaven by a resounding amen from the four creatures, and is further mirrored in the prostration of the twenty-four elders (representing the Old and New Testaments).

## Pointers for prayer

a) The assurance to those in great difficulty is mighty. Have I felt the need of such help? What has it been like?

b) The common prayer of worship can be a terrific source of renewal. Has that ever been my experience, so that I say 'amen' from the heart?

## Prayer

*Faithful God, for all you have done for us in Jesus, we raise a prayer of praise and thanksgiving. Yours is the kingdom, the power and the glory, for ever and ever. Amen!*

## 🌿 First Reading 🌿

**Acts 5:27** When they had brought them, they had them stand before the council. The high priest questioned them, [28] saying, 'We gave you strict orders not to teach in this name, yet here you have filled Jerusalem with your teaching and you are determined to bring this man's blood on us.' [29] But Peter and the apostles answered, 'We must obey God rather than any human authority. [30] The God of our ancestors raised up Jesus, whom you had killed by hanging him on a tree. [31] God exalted him at his right hand as Leader and Saviour that he might give repentance to Israel and forgiveness of sins. [32] And we are witnesses to these things, and so is the Holy Spirit whom God has given to those who obey him.'

[33] *When they heard this, they were enraged and wanted to kill them.* [34] *But a Pharisee in the council named Gamaliel, a teacher of the law, respected by all the people, stood up and ordered the men to be put outside for a short time.* [35] *Then he said to them, "Fellow Israelites, consider carefully what you propose to do to these men.* [36] *For some time ago Theudas rose up, claiming to be somebody, and a number of men, about four hundred, joined him; but he was killed, and all who followed him were dispersed and disappeared.* [37] *After him Judas the Galilean rose up at the time of the census and got people to follow him; he also perished, and all who followed him were scattered.* [38] *So in the present case, I tell you, keep away from these men and let them alone; because if this plan or this undertaking is of human origin, it will fail;* [39] *but if it is of God, you will not be able to overthrow them – in that case you may even be found fighting against God!' They were convinced by him,* [40] *and when they had called in the apostles, they had them flogged.*

Then they ordered them not to speak in the name of Jesus, and let them go. [41] As they left the council, they rejoiced that

they were considered worthy to suffer dishonour for the sake
of the name.

## Initial observations

The lectionary excerpt omits vv. 33–40a for the sake of brevity and, as a result, the decision to release the apostles is not so easy to grasp. For a better understanding, the missing verses are restored here.

## Kind of writing

There are three elements here. Firstly, a story of arrest and defence (frequent in Acts) in vv. 27–28. Secondly, a speech – Peter's fifth, but one of very many Acts – which is in reality a proclamation of the Way, in vv. 29–32. Thirdly, there is a summary statement in vv. 40–42.

## Origin of the reading

Our reading is part of the larger story in Acts 4:24–5:42. There is increasing hostility to the Way. Paradoxically, such antagonism gives rise to increasing courage and 'boldness' (a great early Christian virtue).

## Related Passages

The scene is typical of Acts and a fulfilment of the closing verses of Luke:

> Thus it is written, that the Messiah is to suffer and to rise from the dead on the third day, and that repentance and forgiveness of sins is to be proclaimed in his name to all nations, beginning from Jerusalem. You are witnesses of these things. And see, I am sending upon you what my Father promised; so stay here in the city until you have been clothed with power from on high. (Luke 24:46–49)

> They said, 'What will we do with them? For it is obvious to all who live in Jerusalem that a notable sign has been

done through them; we cannot deny it. But to keep it from
spreading further among the people, let us warn them to
speak no more to anyone in this name.' So they called them
and ordered them not to speak or teach at all in the name of
Jesus. But Peter and John answered them, 'Whether it is right
in God's sight to listen to you rather than to God, you must
judge; for we cannot keep from speaking about what we have
seen and heard.' (Acts 4:16–20)

## Brief commentary

### (V. 27)
A re-arrest has been ordered because the previous gagging order had
been disobeyed and the disciples found themselves again before the
Sanhedrin.

### (V. 28)
Cf. So they called them and ordered them not to speak or teach at all in
the name of Jesus. (Acts 4:18). It is clear historically that, while the Romans actually executed Jesus, it was at the behest of the Jewish leadership. Luke does not blame the people as such, as Matthew seems to do.

### (V. 29)
This is Peter's fifth speech in Acts and it reflect elements already present
in previous orations. The opening statement of principle is very hard to
disagree with. Gamaliel says much the same thing in another way in v.
39.

This principle was by then a Greek proverb of sorts. Cf. Plato *Apology*
29D: I must obey God rather than you. Also in Sophocles, Herodotus,
Epictetus, Athenaeus, Livy and Plutarch.

It is not, however, only classical. It is also found in many biblical passages in the prophets and in the Deuteronomistic writings. Here are examples: Genesis 22:18; Exodus 19:3–6; Deuteronomy 4:30; Jeremiah 3:13
etc. The 'must' is a kind of 'divine necessity' found throughout the Acts.

(V. 30)

God of our ancestors: 3:13. Raised Jesus: Acts 2:24, 32; 3:15. Hanging on a tree: Deuteronomy 21:22–23 – a verse in Paul's mind too when he wrote, Christ redeemed us from the curse of the law by becoming a curse for us – for it is written, 'Cursed is everyone who hangs on a tree' – in order that in Christ Jesus the blessing of Abraham might come to the Gentiles, so that we might receive the promise of the Spirit through faith (Galatians 3:13–14).

(V. 31)

Exalted: Being therefore exalted at the right hand of God, and having received from the Father the promise of the Holy Spirit, he has poured out this that you both see and hear (Acts 2:33). Repentance and forgiveness of sins: Luke 3:3; 17:3; 24:47; Acts 2:38; 8:38.

(V. 32)

Witnesses: Acts 2:32; 3:15. Holy Spirit: Acts 2:33 and forty-two other occurrences in the Acts. Obedience: 'Blessed rather are those who hear the word of God and obey it!' (Luke 11:28).

(V. 40b)

Yes, but not before having them flogged. Cf. Acts 4:18; 9:27. Vv. 40–42 form a summary statement, the fifth so far in the Acts.

(V. 41)

Joy in suffering for the name is the mark of messianic communities: Acts 8:8; 11:23; 13:48, 52; 15:3, 31; 16:34. For example, He brought them up into the house and set food before them; and he and his entire household rejoiced that he had become a believer in God (Acts 16:34).

## Pointers for prayer

a) Has it ever been my experience to be under pressure for being a believer? How did I react? Did I flinch? Did I 'go under'? Did I grow?

b) Choosing God rather than human authority could be a life-changing choice: has such a stark option been my experience?

## Prayer

*God, you raised Jesus from the dead and gave us life in his name. As we bear the name of Christian, help us to follow Jesus not only in name but also in fact. Give us the courage to bear witness and the boldness to speak out. Through Christ our Lord. Amen.*

## Themes across the readings

The same figure – Peter – is dominant in both Acts and John. In the gospel, we see traces of the old Peter, in need of repentance, forgiveness and reconciliation. In the Acts, we see the new Peter, marked (mostly, not always!) by courage. Psalm 30 (29), after the Acts, fits the story of pressure and release really well. The first two lines say it all: *I will praise you, Lord, you have rescued me and have not let my enemies rejoice over me.*

# Chapter 4

## Easter 4C

## Thought for the day

The cultural dismissal of faith as illusory consolation or opium has left its mark on us all. Is it all projection? Has God truly spoken and revealed God's self? In Christian faith, our response is a resounding yes, and while we should be wary of facile solace, at the same time we should not deny ourselves the good and wholesome reassurance of faith. After all, one of the most repeated phrases throughout the Bible is 'Do not be afraid' (though not in John, curiously). There are grounds for fear; but we, of all people, should not be overwhelmed by the negative.

## Prayer

*Lord Jesus, risen from the dead, guide us to listen deeply to your voice, your word, that we may know you and, that knowing you, we may enjoy life in abundance, now and into eternity with you, who live and reign for ever and ever. Amen.*

## 🌿 Gospel 🌿

**Jn 10:22** At that time the festival of the Dedication took place in Jerusalem. It was winter, 23 and Jesus was walking in the temple, in the portico of Solomon. 24 So the Jews gathered around him and said to him, 'How long will you keep us in suspense? If you are the Messiah, tell us plainly.' 25 Jesus answered, 'I have told you, and you do not believe. The works that I do in my Father's name testify to me; 26 but you

> do not believe, because you do not belong to my sheep. [27] My sheep hear my voice. I know them, and they follow me. [28] I give them eternal life, and they will never perish. No one will snatch them out of my hand. [29] What my Father has given me is greater than all else, and no one can snatch it out of the Father's hand. [30] The Father and I are one.'

## Initial observations

This reading (vv. 27–30) is probably the shortest gospel reading on any Sunday. Nevertheless, it is deeply resonant, especially when read in the light of the same words and images elsewhere in the Fourth Gospel. As a result, it repays close and careful reading.

The rather controversial setting is apparent from the introductory verses, added here to give the context. This is not unimportant because the controversy over the identity of Jesus leads to his death, precisely as the shepherd who lays down his life for the sheep. V. 30 is key, therefore.

## Kind of writing

The passage comes from a new section in the gospel. Jesus is in Jerusalem for the feast of Dedication (Hanukkah), which occurs in late November or in December. The imagery of shepherd, however, takes us back to the previous Good Shepherd discourse from 10:1ff. and should be read in light of that. The question asked in v. 24 is the core question of the whole gospel: Who is Jesus? The answer given in v. 30 is, in this gospel, the cause of Jesus' death.

## Old Testament background

Across the ancient Near East, rulers were regularly called shepherds, on account of the pivotal role of the pastor in the care of the sheep. It was the shepherd's responsibility to protect, guide and feed, as it was that of a monarch. It is no surprise that likewise people called their 'god' a shepherd, well before and outside of the biblical use of the metaphor. That said, the biblical tradition makes very rich use of this imagery.

(i) A Psalm of David. The Lord is my shepherd, I shall not want. He makes me lie down in green pastures; he leads me beside still waters; he restores my soul. He leads me in right paths for his name's sake. Even though I walk through the darkest valley, I fear no evil; for you are with me; your rod and your staff – they comfort me. You prepare a table before me in the presence of my enemies; you anoint my head with oil; my cup overflows. Surely goodness and mercy shall follow me all the days of my life, and I shall dwell in the house of the Lord my whole life long. (Psalm 23:1–6)

(ii) For thus says the Lord God: I myself will search for my sheep, and will seek them out. As shepherds seek out their flocks when they are among their scattered sheep, so I will seek out my sheep. I will rescue them from all the places to which they have been scattered on a day of clouds and thick darkness. I will bring them out from the peoples and gather them from the countries, and will bring them into their own land; and I will feed them on the mountains of Israel, by the watercourses, and in all the inhabited parts of the land. I will feed them with good pasture, and the mountain heights of Israel shall be their pasture; there they shall lie down in good grazing land, and they shall feed on rich pasture on the mountains of Israel. I myself will be the shepherd of my sheep, and I will make them lie down, says the Lord God. I will seek the lost, and I will bring back the strayed, and I will bind up the injured, and I will strengthen the weak, but the fat and the strong I will destroy. I will feed them with justice. (Ezekiel 34:11–16)

## New Testament foreground

The Fourth Gospel often builds its distinctive reflections on foundations taken from the Synoptic tradition. This is the case here.

(i) As he went ashore, Jesus saw a great crowd; and he had compassion for them, because they were like sheep without a shepherd; and he began to teach them many things. (Mark 6:34)

(ii) 'And you, Bethlehem, in the land of Judah, are by no means least among the rulers of Judah; for from you shall come a ruler who is to shepherd my people Israel.' (Matthew 2:6)

(iii) So he told them this parable: 'Which one of you, having a hundred sheep and losing one of them, does not leave the ninety-nine in the wilderness and go after the one that is lost until he finds it? When he has found it, he lays it on his shoulders and rejoices. And when he comes home, he calls together his friends and neighbours, saying to them: "Rejoice with me, for I have found my sheep that was lost." Just so, I tell you, there will be more joy in heaven over one sinner who repents than over ninety-nine righteous persons who need no repentance.' (Luke 15:3–7)

(iv) 'I am the good shepherd. The good shepherd lays down his life for the sheep. The hired hand, who is not the shepherd and does not own the sheep, sees the wolf coming and leaves the sheep and runs away – and the wolf snatches them and scatters them. The hired hand runs away because a hired hand does not care for the sheep. I am the good shepherd.

'I know my own and my own know me, just as the Father knows me and I know the Father. And I lay down my life for the sheep. I have other sheep that do not belong to this fold. I must bring them also, and they will listen to my voice. So there will be one flock, one shepherd. For this reason the Father loves me, because I lay down my life in order to take it up again. No one takes it from me, but I lay it down of my own accord. I have power to lay it down, and I have power to take it up again. I have received this command from my Father.' (John 10:11–18)

(v) When they had finished breakfast, Jesus said to Simon Peter, 'Simon son of John, do you love me more than these?' He said to him, 'Yes, Lord; you know that I love you.' Jesus said to him, 'Feed my lambs.' A second time he said to him, 'Simon son of John, do you love me?' He said to him, 'Yes, Lord; you know that I love you.' Jesus said to him, 'Tend my sheep.' He said to him the third time, 'Simon son of John, do you love me?' Peter felt hurt because he said to him the third time, 'Do you love me?' And he said to him, 'Lord, you know everything; you know that I love you.' Jesus said to him, 'Feed my sheep. (John 21:15–17)

## St Paul

The life I now live in the body, I live because of the faithfulness of the Son of God, who loved me and gave himself for me. (Galatians 2:20)

For our paschal lamb, Christ, has been sacrificed. (1 Corinthians 5:7)

## Brief commentary

(V. 22-23)
The feast of Dedication governs the rest of John 10. After the destruction of the Temple, all Jewish traditions, including the Nazarene sect, wondered about the place of encounter with God. Christians did not locate it in a place or a book but in a person. See John 4:23.

(V. 24)
This question is both odd and typical. It is odd in John's Gospel because throughout Jesus has been open about his identity. Typical because Jesus is the total focus of this gospel.

(Vv. 25–26)
This is markedly robust and reflects conflicts at the time of writing between the Johannine community and the synagogue 'across the road'. To believe is huge in this gospel: the verb occurs no fewer than ninety-eight times.

(V. 27)

The Good Shepherd is speaking. Voice: When he had said this, he cried with a loud voice, 'Lazarus, come out!' (John 11:43). Jesus said to her, 'Mary!' (John 20:16). Jesus said to him, 'Feed my sheep' (John 21:17). 'Follow' takes us back to the earliest call of Jesus in the gospels (John 1:37–38, 40, 43), echoed in John 21: 'After this he said to him, "Follow me"' (John 21:19).

(V. 28)

In the Fourth Gospel, eternal life does not mean only or even primarily life after death. It means instead that quality of authentic life, which the believer already has now through faith in Jesus. 'For God so loved the world that he gave his only Son, so that everyone who believes in him may not perish but may have eternal life' (John 3:16). 'Very truly, I tell you, anyone who hears my word and believes him who sent me has eternal life, and does not come under judgment, but has passed from death to life' (John 5:24). 'Very truly, I tell you, whoever believes has eternal life' (John 6:47). 'And this is eternal life, that they may know you, the only true God, and Jesus Christ whom you have sent' (John 17:3). 'The followers of Jesus are protected: While I was with them, I protected them in your name that you have given me' (John 17:12).

(V. 29)

Given: 'Now they know that everything you have given me is from you; for the words that you gave to me I have given to them, and they have received them and know in truth that I came from you; and they have believed that you sent me' (John 17:7–8). And during supper Jesus, knowing that the Father had given all things into his hands, and that he had come from God and was going to God … (John 13:2–4).

(V. 30)

That oneness between the Father and the Son is offered to all believers as well: 'I ask not only on behalf of these, but also on behalf of those who will believe in me through their word, that they may all be one. As you, Father, are in me and I am in you, may they also be in us, so that the world may believe that you have sent me. The glory that you have given me I have given them, so that they may be one, as we are one, I in them and you in me, that they may become completely one, so that the world may know that you have sent me and have loved them even as you have loved me' (John 17:20–24).

## Pointers for prayer

a) Jesus tells us that we can rely on his relationship with us. Think of the relationships you have in which you feel safe and secure because there is mutual understanding and the relationship has stood the test of time.

b) Jesus says that the disciple is one who listens. What is your experience of listening to the word of God in the Scriptures? To what other voices have you listened and found guidance?

c) The faithful disciple is also one who follows the path of love that Jesus preached and practised. Although it may be difficult at times, it is in following it that we find life. Where have you had the experience of listening, responding, loving and finding life?

## Prayer

*Safe in your hands, O God, is the flock you shepherd through Jesus your Son. Lead us always to the living waters where you promise respite and refreshment, that we may be counted among those who know and follow you. We ask this through Jesus Christ, the resurrection and the life, who lives and reigns with you in the unity of the Holy Spirit God for ever and ever. Amen.*

## 🌿 Second Reading 🌿

**Rev 7:9** After this I looked, and there was a great multitude that no one could count, from every nation, from all tribes and peoples and languages, standing before the throne and before the Lamb, robed in white, with palm branches in their hands. [10] They cried out in a loud voice, saying,

'Salvation belongs to our God who is seated on the

throne, and to the Lamb!'
[11] And all the angels stood around the throne and around the elders and the four living creatures, and they fell on their faces before the throne and worshipped God, [12] singing,

> 'Amen! Blessing and glory and wisdom and
> thanksgiving and honour and power and might be
> to our God for ever and ever! Amen.'

[13] Then one of the elders addressed me, saying, 'Who are these, robed in white, and where have they come from?' [14] I said to him, 'Sir, you are the one that knows.' Then he said to me, 'These are they who have come out of the great ordeal; they have washed their robes and made them white in the blood of the Lamb.

[15] For this reason they are before the throne of God,
> and worship him day and night
within his temple,
> and the one who is seated on the
throne will shelter them.
[16] They will hunger no more, and thirst no more;
> the sun will not strike them,
> nor any scorching heat;
[17] for the Lamb at the centre of the throne
will be their shepherd,
> and he will guide them to springs of the water of life,
and God will wipe away every tear from their eyes.'

## Initial observations

Fortunately, the lectionary offers us some of the less forbidding scenes from the Apocalypse. Today's reading, to some degree, uses images and metaphors not too remote or esoteric. A good link with today's gospel is found in v. 17: for the Lamb at the centre of the throne will be their shepherd, and he will guide them to springs of the water of life. In the end, the writer is basing everything on Jesus' death and resurrection and, at the same time, proclaiming the future salvation of all who believe and hold fast.

## Kind of writing

Where are we in the Apocalypse? An outline of the book may help us.

Prologue 1:1–3
Epistolary prescript 1:4–6
Prophetic sayings 1:7–8

Visionary report 1:9–22:5
I. Epiphany of the risen Christ 1:9–3:22
The seven messages 2:1–3:22
II. Vision in the spirit 4:1–22:5
The scroll with seven seals 6:1–11:19
    The first six seals 6:1–17
    The 144,000 7:1–17
    The seventh seal 8:1–11:19
The open scroll 12:1–22:5
    The woman 12:1–18
    Chaos unleashed 13:1–18
    End-time vision 14:1–20
    The seven bowls 15:1–16:20
    Vision of Babylon 17:1–19:10
    The last things 19:11–20:21
    Vision of Jerusalem 21:9–22:5
Prophetic sayings 22:6–20
Epistolary concluding blessing 22:21

Our reading comes from second major section, precisely from the section devoted to the 144,000 in vv. 7:1–17. This is a consoling vision before the Seventh Seal is opened, unleashing the forces of evil. It is designed to bolster or buttress the faith of the persecuted.

## Origin of the reading

The setting in the community is the need to strengthen and sustain believers at a time of immense pressure. No doubt many departed from the community and some are wondering why or even how they can remain.

Not at all unlike our own times, really. The preceding vv. 1–8 give greater detail about this vast multitude. Again, the inclusion of hymns familiar to the community (vv. 10, 12) promotes identification with the message.

## Related Passages

> After this I saw four angels standing at the four corners of the earth, holding back the four winds of the earth so that no wind could blow on earth or sea or against any tree. I saw another angel ascending from the rising of the sun, having the seal of the living God, and he called with a loud voice to the four angels who had been given power to damage earth and sea, saying, 'Do not damage the earth or the sea or the trees, until we have marked the servants of our God with a seal on their foreheads.'

> And I heard the number of those who were sealed, one hundred forty-four thousand, sealed out of every tribe of the people of Israel. (Revelation 7:1–4)

## Brief commentary

(V. 9)
From the number that no one could count, it is clear that 144,000 is symbolic (144 by 1000). The fourfold designation indicates all of creation. The throne indicates God's power while the Lamb emphasises God's paradoxical rule through vulnerability. White is the colour of resurrection and palms are a symbol of victory.

(Vv. 10–14a)
The hymn (not in our reading) is the clue to the status of these people, already singing of victory.

(V. 14bc)
An interpretive word is required. These are the victorious believers, who have survived the end-time upheaval. Washing in blood (not a known

detergent) illustrates the use of clashing symbolism. The robes indicate the inner person, rendered pure by faith in Jesus' death and resurrection.

(V. 15)
Because they have come through, these saints stand eternally before God. See Ezekiel 37:27.

(V. 16)
Cf. They shall not hunger or thirst, neither scorching wind nor sun shall strike them down, for he who has pity on them will lead them, and by springs of water will guide them (Isaiah 49:10). Also: John 4, throughout.

(V. 17)
Cf. Then the Lord God will wipe away the tears from all faces, and the disgrace of his people he will take away from all the earth, for the Lord has spoken (Isaiah 25:8).

## Pointers for prayer

a) Perhaps we hesitate these days to inhabit fully the reassurance of faith – but why not?

b) Are you experiencing some 'great ordeal' right now? Or even in the past? Where is your source of strength?

## Prayer

*Mysterious God, we call you by many names: love, mercy, compassion, kindness and hope. Draw us ever more closely into the circle of your life that our faith may be strong and our hope a source of well-being and vigour. Through Christ our Lord. Amen.*

## 🌿 First Reading 🌿

**Acts 13:13** *Then Paul and his companions set sail from Paphos and came to Perga in Pamphylia. John, however, left them and returned to Jerusalem;* [14] *but they went on from Perga and came to Antioch in Pisidia. And on the sabbath day they went into the synagogue and sat down.*

⁴³ When the meeting of the synagogue broke up, many Jews and devout converts to Judaism followed Paul and Barnabas, who spoke to them and urged them to continue in the grace of God.

⁴⁴ The next Sabbath almost the whole city gathered to hear the word of the Lord. ⁴⁵ But when the Jews saw the crowds, they were filled with jealousy; and blaspheming, they contradicted what was spoken by Paul. ⁴⁶ Then both Paul and Barnabas spoke out boldly, saying, 'It was necessary that the word of God should be spoken first to you. Since you reject it and judge yourselves to be unworthy of eternal life, we are now turning to the Gentiles. ⁴⁷ For so the Lord has commanded us, saying,

"I have set you to be a light for the Gentiles, so that
you may bring salvation to the ends of the earth."'

⁴⁸ When the Gentiles heard this, they were glad and praised the word of the Lord; and as many as had been destined for eternal life became believers. ⁴⁹ Thus the word of the Lord spread throughout the region. ⁵⁰ But the Jews incited the devout women of high standing and the leading men of the city, and stirred up persecution against Paul and Barnabas, and drove them out of their region. ⁵¹ So they shook the dust off their feet in protest against them, and went to Iconium. ⁵² And the disciples were filled with joy and with the Holy Spirit.

## Initial observations

For our notes, v.13 has been added to give the immediate context. The story told today is typical of the Acts, where, upon rejection by the Jews, the missionaries of the Way turn to the Gentiles. The reading has a fairly large gap in it (we jumped from v.14 to 43!), so it would be good to read the intervening verses to make sense of the excerpt. The speech is a substantial presentation of the Way. It is programmatic in the same way as Peter's speech on Pentecost (Acts 2:14–41) and Jesus' sermon in Nazareth (Luke 4:16–30).

# Kind of writing

The main burden of the excerpt is given over to reactions to the speech of Paul, both positive and negative. This is also programmatic, as we can see in many other passages, such as Acts 16:14, 17:4, 17; 18:7 etc.

## Origin of the reading

Luke groups the missionary activities in three blocks, traditionally known as the Missionary Journeys:

| I | 13:1–14:28 |
|---|---|
| II | 15:36–18:22 |
| III | 18:23–21:16 |

As there is no confirmation of the first missionary journey in the letters of Paul, some scholars think it is a complete invention by Luke. In any case, our reading reflects a missionary journey, of evidently limited scope.

## Related passages

The pattern of speaking 'the word of God' first in the synagogues is found throughout the Acts: Antioch (13:14), Iconium (14:1); Thessalonica (17:1); Berea (17:10); Athens 17:17; Corinth (18:4); Ephesus (18:19; 19:8) in the case of Paul. Apollos likewise in Ephesus (18:26).

## Brief commentary

(V. 14)
This takes place, naturally, in Antioch in Pisidia, on a Sabbath. The great speech of Paul follows here. The missing speech is heard on Thursday and Friday this coming week.

(V. 43)
The devout converts are, of course, Gentiles, most likely taken from the god-fearers. On the grace of God, see 2:47.

(V. 44)
The word of God is a key expression in the Acts (Acts 4:31; 6:2, 7; 8:14;

11:1; 12:24; 13:5, 7, 46; 17:13; 18:11). Luke has a tendency to overstate, so the whole city might be taken with a pinch of salt.

(V. 45)
This highly negative reaction is also found elsewhere: the priests in Jerusalem (5:17); the Jews in Thessalonica (17:5); the Jews in Rome (28:19, 22).

(V. 46)
Speaking frankly or boldly is typical of Paul in Acts: see 28:31. The necessity of speaking in the synagogues first is interpreted as a divine necessity. The turning to the Gentiles marks subsequent episodes in Acts: Corinth (18:6); Ephesus (19:9) and Rome (28:28). 'Judging yourselves unworthy' is highly ironic in the context.

(V. 47)
The turning to the Gentiles is by no means a second best, but follows the command of the Lord. The citation that follows has already been spoken elsewhere. Light to the Gentiles: spoken by Simeon in Luke 2:32. Salvation to the ends of the earth: spoken by the risen Lord in Acts 1:8. It is not, however, to take the place of a mission to the Jews, because the rest of the citation on Simeon's lips reads 'and for glory to your people Israel' (Luke 2:32).

(V. 48)
Rejoicing is typical of believers in Acts (13:53; 15:3; 5:41), as is praising the word of the Lord (11:18).

(V. 49)
A summary statement, based on previous experiences in Caesarea (10:45) and Jerusalem (11:18).

(V. 50)
This is a very different reaction, perhaps based on the demanding citizenship oaths typically undertaken by inhabitants of the empire.

(V.51)
Shaking the dust: cf. Iconium (14:2) and Corinth (18:6). In the Old Testament, dust is a signal of divine punishment.

(V. 52)

In some contrast (!), the disciples head away full of joy (5:41; 8:8; 11:23) and the Holy Spirit (4:8 and many other places).

## Pointers for prayer

a) It can happen, when we do our best, that people react in different ways. Have I had such experiences? What was it like? How did I react to that?

b) Negative situations sometimes turn out to be new opportunities, as in this reading. Can I recall any situation which looked like an unmitigated disaster, but which in retrospect turned out to be a grace?

c) Reacting in knee-jerk fashion, with jealousy etc., is not unknown and may well be part of my own experience. What have I learned?

## Prayer

*O God, it is your word we hear. Help us to learn from every experience, both good and bad, and let us put our joyful trust in your Holy Spirit. Through Christ our Lord. Amen.*

## Themes across the readings

In our first reading the conviction and commitment of the apostles are under threat – something that we find also in the second reading. Both readings point to Jesus and faith in him, the great topic of the gospel today. Notice the key words: salvation (Acts), living water (Apocalypse) and eternal life (John). The psalm is a general invitation to all the nations to worship God and so it matches the reading well. The response, in particular, looks forward to the gospel.

# Chapter 5

## Easter 5C

## Thought for the day

According to the song 'Nature Boy', 'the greatest thing you'll ever learn is to love and be loved in return.' In our better moments, we all know this to be the truth about our human being. For believers, it is no surprise that the very thing we need most stands at the centre of the Christian faith: God is love. The match between our need and God's disclosure is perfect. If we took that really to heart, many things would change: our practice of prayer, our relationships, our joy in believing, our way of sharing our faith, our living of discipleship. All we need is love. The astonishing servant love of God in Jesus is exactly what we most need.

## Prayer

*You are love itself and yet we hesitate. Open our inner selves to your gracious loving, that we may see ourselves as beloved and, being loved, we may learn to love in return. We ask this through Christ our Lord. Amen.*

## 🌾 Gospel 🌿

**Jn 13:31** When Judas had gone out, Jesus said, 'Now the Son of Man has been glorified, and God has been glorified in him. [32] If God has been glorified in him, God will also glorify him in himself and will glorify him at once. [33] Little children, I am with you only a little longer. You will look for me; and as I said to the Jews so now I say to you, 'Where I am going, you cannot come.' [34] I give you a new commandment, that you love one another. Just as I have loved you, you also should love one another. [35] By this everyone will know that you are my disciples, if you have love for one another.'

## Initial observations

The commandment to love God and your neighbour, taken from the Hebrew Bible, is given by Jesus in Mark 12 as the 'greatest commandment'. Our text today reflects the reception of this tradition in the Johannine community and literature, where it receives a unique profile.

## Kind of writing

In the Fourth Gospel, chs 14–17 belong to the literary genre of the final speech of the hero, his or her last will and testament. The farewell speech is well established as a literary genre in the OT and the apocryphal books of the intertestamental period. There are numerous examples, like the blessings of Jacob to his children in Genesis 47:29–49:33, the farewell of Joshua to the nation of Israel in Joshua 22–24, and David's farewell speech in 1 Chronicles 28–29. In the Old Testament apocrypha we have the farewell speech of Tobit from his deathbed in Tobit 14:3–11. The entire *Testaments of the Twelve Patriarchs* is made up of farewell speeches patterned after Jacob's speech in Genesis. The *Book of Jubilees* gives farewell speeches for Noah (ch. 10), Abraham (chs 20–22), and Rebecca and Isaac (chs 35–36). Josephus includes a farewell address for Moses. In the New Testament, Paul makes a farewell speech to the elders at Ephesus in Acts 20:17–38, and the Pastoral Epistles in their entirety might be thought of as farewells, especially 2 Timothy. Correspondingly, 2 Peter is cast in the form of Peter's farewell discourse.

The common situation in almost all of these instances is that of a prominent person who gathers his followers (children, disciples or the entire nation of Israel) just before his death or departure to give them final instructions, which will help them after he is gone.

In our passage, Jesus speaks of his death (glorification in this gospel) and how the 'little children' are to love one another after he has gone. The material in John 14–17 is, of course, not historical, but gives us the fruit of profound meditation on the deep meaning of Jesus, as disclosed to the Johannine community, through the great religious genius who was its founder and guide.

## Old Testament background

There are three Old Testament backgrounds to this passage.

(i) Glory refers to God's presence in the Temple, which was both immanent (here and now) and transcendent (beyond). One example: 'Then the cloud covered the tent of meeting, and the glory of the Lord filled the tabernacle. Moses was not able to enter the tent of meeting because the cloud settled upon it, and the glory of the Lord filled the tabernacle' (Exodus 40:34–35).

(ii) Son of Man is a term taken from the book of Daniel where it refers not simply to a human being (the usual meaning) but to the agent of God's final salvation to all humanity. In this sense, it was definitely used by the historical Jesus in reference to himself.

As I watched in the night visions, I saw one like a Son of Man (the NRSV gets this wrong) coming with the clouds of heaven. And he came to the Ancient One and was presented before him. (Daniel 7:13)

(iii) Love as the great commandment is given in Deuteronomy (the Shema Yisrael) and Leviticus: 'Hear, O Israel: The Lord is our God, the Lord alone. You shall love the Lord your God with all your heart, and with all your soul, and with all your might' (Deuteronomy 6:4–5). 'You shall not take vengeance or bear a grudge against any of your people, but you shall love your neighbour as yourself: I am the Lord' (Leviticus 19:18).

All three references are significant: God's glory is now shown in the final love of Jesus, in his lifting up on the cross into resurrection, making him the saviour; by his gift of himself we are enabled to love just as he loved.

## New Testament foreground

(i) 'To glorify' is used in the Fourth Gospel to refer to the revelation of God's inner self, which will be brought about by the death and resurrection of Jesus (his lifting up). As we saw above, the term can also mean God's immanence and transcendence in the incarnate Word (who 'tented among us', whose 'glory we have seen'). The hour of glory is announced by Jesus in John 12:23: Jesus answered them, 'The hour has come for the Son of Man to be glorified.'

(ii) The historical Jesus summarised the commandments into two, love of God and love of neighbour, in Mark 12:28–34 (and parallels in Matthew 22:34–40 and Luke 10:25–28). This summary is echoed widely across New Testament documents. For example: 'You do well if you really fulfil the royal law according to the scripture, "You shall love your neighbour as yourself"' (James 2:8; several times in Paul – see below).

(iii) In the Fourth Gospel itself, the command to love is given a high profile, so that it becomes really the only ethical requirement of the community: Matthew (x8), Mark (x5), Luke (x13), John (x37). The formulation to love one another recurs in John 15:12, 17, in 1 John 3:11, 23; 4:7, 11–13 and in 2 John 5.

## St Paul

The commandments, 'You shall not commit adultery; You shall not murder; You shall not steal; You shall not covet'; and any other commandment, are summed up in this word, 'Love your neighbour as yourself.' (Romans 13:9)

For the whole law is summed up in a single commandment, 'You shall love your neighbour as yourself.' (Galatians 5:14)

## Brief commentary

(V. 31)

The departure of Judas is the signal for a more direct and essential teaching to the disciples. Notice the past tense – we are dealing with a Johannine expression of faith from the end of the first century AD. Jesus, the agent of God's final salvation, has been lifted up on the cross (John 3) and, in the lifting up, God's own 'glory', his loving inner self, was revealed.

(V. 32)

The tense changes from the past (the point of view of the faith community) to the future (the point of view of Jesus' giving his last will and testament). 'At once' (only x3 in John) is used again at the cross: 'at once, blood and water flowed out'.

(V. 33)

'Little children', a term taken from the Johannine community (x1 in John, here, and x7 in 1 John), is especially affectionate. 'Looking for' Jesus has been a feature of this gospel from the start. 'Going': cf. Jesus then said, 'I will be with you a little while longer, and then I am going to him who sent me. You will search for me, but you will not find me; and where I am, you cannot come' (John 7:33–34). Again he said to them, 'I am going away, and you will search for me, but you will die in your sin. Where I am going, you cannot come' (John 8:21).

(V. 34)

New commandment: cf. John 15:12, 17. The writer knows this commandment is both new and old (from Deuteronomy and Leviticus): Beloved, I am writing you no new commandment, but an old commandment that you have had from the beginning; the old commandment is the word that you have heard. Yet I am writing you a new commandment that is true in him and in you, because the darkness is passing away and the true light is already shining (1 John 2:7–8). It is old in its form. It is new in the Christian dispensation, because of the radical depth of love shown in Christ, which also makes the commandment (newly) possible in an absolutely new way. The tiny expression 'just as' is vital here. As elsewhere in this gospel (John 20:21), it means more than 'on the model of Jesus'; rather, by means of Jesus' loving us or on the strength of Jesus' love, we are enabled to love as he loved.

(V. 35)

The insistence on love as the distinguishing mark of the Christian is found extensively in the New Testament. As is well known, there are three expressions for love in Greek: *philia* (friendship); *eros* (attraction between the sexes); *agapē* (unrestricted, indiscriminate seeking of the other's well-being, without expectation of reward). See Benedict XVI's encyclical, *God Is Love. Agapē*, the last above, is used in the New Testament in a distinctively Christian way. Of course, behind the idealisation lies the reality that the Johannine community, full of tensions and splits, needed to hear this commandment again and again (as we do too!).

## Pointers for prayer

a) Judas leaves and Jesus announces that the moment has come for God's power to be made manifest. This is unexpected at a moment of imminent betrayal. Have there been times for you when the power of God was made manifest in strange circumstances?

b) 'I shall not be with you much longer.' Jesus announces a parting of the ways. There are places we have to go in life where others cannot come with us. There are places others have to go and we cannot accompany them. When have you experienced this going on alone as necessary for a fuller life for yourself, or for someone else?

c) Jesus proclaims love as the distinguishing characteristic of his followers. Have there been times when reaching out to others has heightened your sense of walking in the footsteps of Jesus?

d) Who are the individuals or communities whose love for one another and for others has been a witness to you?

## Prayer

*We behold your glory, in the love shown by your Son, lifted up on the cross and exalted on high. Increase our love for one another, that both in name and in truth we may be disciples of the risen Lord Jesus and so reflect in our lives the glory that is yours.*

*We ask this through Christ, the first-born from the dead, who lives and reigns with you in the unity of the Holy Spirit, God for ever and ever. Amen.*

## ❧ Second Reading ❧

**Rev 21:1** Then I saw a new heaven and a new earth; for the first heaven and the first earth had passed away, and the sea was no more. ² And I saw the holy city, the new Jerusalem, coming down out of heaven from God, prepared as a bride adorned for her husband. ³ And I heard a loud voice from the throne saying,

'See, the home of God is among mortals.
He will dwell with them;
they will be his peoples,
and God himself will be with them; ⁴
he will wipe every tear from their eyes.
Death will be no more;
mourning and crying and pain will be no more,
for the first things have passed away.'

⁵ And the one who was seated on the throne said, 'See, I am making all things new.' Also he said, 'Write this, for these words are trustworthy and true.'

## Initial observations

The Apocalypse can be a very difficult book. Fortunately, the final chapters are extraordinarily poetic and uplifting. The words go straight to the heart of the matter and to the heart of the human condition.

## Kind of writing

In terms of the overall book, we find ourselves in the final vision of the new Jerusalem. Today, we read the first part of that vision (the full outline is in ch. 3).

II. Vision in the spirit 4:1–22:5
The open scroll 12:1–22:5
    The woman 12:1–18
    Chaos unleashed 13:1–18
    End-time vision 14:1–20
    The seven bowls 15:1–16:20
    Vision of Babylon 17:1–19:10
    The last things 19:11–20:21
    Vision of Jerusalem 21:1–22:5

## Origin of the reading

The context in the community is the time after the destruction of the actual city of Jerusalem, a time marked by a certain alienation or home-lessness. The convictions of the believers made them feel not at all 'at home' in the empire. The final chapters are full of references to the Old Testament, already regarded as the Word of God, thus lending tremen-dous authority to the final affirmations.

## Related passages

We note here the related passages from the Hebrew Bible, essential as a key to what the writer is teaching. A sample text is given for each set of references, to when the appetite of the reader.

*New heaven and new earth:* Isaiah 65:17–19; 66:22.

> For I am about to create new heavens and a new earth; the former things shall not be remembered or come to mind. But be glad and rejoice forever in what I am creating; for I am about to create Jerusalem as a joy, and its people as a delight. I will rejoice in Jerusalem, and delight in my people;

no more shall the sound of weeping be heard in it, or the cry of distress. (Isaiah 65:17–19)

*As a bride:* Isaiah 49:18; 52:1; 54:4–6; 61:10; 62:4–5 etc.

Do not fear, for you will not be ashamed; do not be discouraged, for you will not suffer disgrace; for you will forget the shame of your youth, and the disgrace of your widowhood you will remember no more. For your Maker is your husband, the LORD of hosts is his name; the Holy One of Israel is your Redeemer, the God of the whole earth he is called. For the LORD has called you like a wife forsaken and grieved in spirit, like the wife of a man's youth when she is cast off, says your God. (Isaiah 54:4–6)

*God's home:* Exodus 6:7; 25:8; 29:45; Leviticus 26:11–12; 1 Kings 6:13; Ezekiel 37:27; 43:7; Zechariah 2:14; 8:8; 13:9.

And have them make me a sanctuary, so that I may dwell among them. (Exodus 25:8)

*Tears:* Isaiah 25:8; 30:19; 35:10; 51:11; 60:20; 61:3; 65:18–19; Jeremiah 31:12–13; Hosea 13:14.

Then the LORD GOD will wipe away the tears from all faces, and the disgrace of his people he will take away from all the earth, for the LORD has spoken. (Isaiah 25:8)

*Things new:* Psalm 104:30; Isaiah 42:9; 43:19; 48:6; 65:17; Ezekiel 36:26.

*Write this:* Habakkuk 2:2.

Then the LORD answered me and said: Write the vision; make it plain on tablets, so that a runner may read it. (Habakkuk 2:2)

The prophets were clearly important for this writer, especially Isaiah, the 'fifth evangelist'.'

## Brief commentary

**(V. 1)**

The brusque dissolution of the first heaven and the first earth might seem to augur ill for a theology of care of creation. It is, however, figurative, and the text speaks rather of the end-time renewal of creation and the fulfilment of prophecies such as those of Isaiah above. This radical transformation of the cosmos includes the radical transformation of its inhabitants too. Such a root and branch renewal had already started in the resurrection of Jesus, understood as the first instalment of the end-time realities.

The sea, too, is figurative. In the Apocalypse it refers to the forces of chaos and death, in four senses: (i) the origin of cosmic evil; (ii) unbelieving people; (iii) the place of the dead; (iv) the location of idolatrous imperial trade. The metaphorical disappearance of the sea means that the vanquishing of evil will be absolute. Thus the sea will not be any longer just as death will not be no more.

**(V. 2)**

This new metaphor comes from Isaiah 52:1–10. The nuptial imagery has a wide basis in the Old Testament. Cf. Isaiah 62:1–10. The 'holy city' is also taken from Isaiah 62. The descent of the new creation brings about the replacement of the old. Cf. Galatians 4:26–31; Hebrews 12:22 cf. Philippians 3:20; also in Jewish apocalyptic writings such as 4 *Ezra* 7:26; 10:25–27, 41–44, 49–55; 2 *Enoch* 55:2. Behind the imagery stands God's promise of final salvation and righteousness.

**(V. 3)**

Symbolically, this proclamation comes from God himself. The biblical allusions (above) are echoes especially of Ezekiel and his image of the end-time temple, in which God will dwell among the children of Israel for ever. Cf. I will make a covenant of peace with them; it shall be an everlasting covenant with them; and I will bless them and multiply them, and will set my sanctuary among them forever more. My dwelling place shall be with them; and I will be their God, and they shall be my people. Then the nations shall know that I the Lord sanctify Israel, when my sanctuary is among them for ever more (Ezekiel 37:26–28). This time, however, the divine presence or Shekhinah is not limited to any physical temple.

(V. 4)

Total peace and relief are promised, based on key citations from the Old Testament. Then the LORD GOD will wipe away the tears from all faces, and the disgrace of his people he will take away from all the earth, for the LORD has spoken (Isaiah 25:8). For I am about to create new heavens and a new earth; the former things shall not be remembered or come to mind (Isaiah 65:17).

(V. 5)

This verse starts a wider discussion in vv. 5–8. Note that the author adds the word 'all' to indicate that the fulfilment of Isaiah is complete. A title for Jesus in the Apocalypse is 'the faithful and true witness', echoed here in the message from the throne. Utter reliability, total faithfulness!

## Pointers for prayer

a)  God is, in the words of Bonhoeffer, 'the beyond in the midst'. What is your experience of the nearness of the Mystery?

b)  Our text contains unlimited reassurance – quite remarkably unrestricted. Such grace is ours to embrace, to enjoy, to live.

## Prayer

*God of surprises, surprise us again with your vision of future life and new hope. We need your message as never before. Overcome our hesitation and help us to embrace your faithful love to all. Through Christ our Lord. Amen.*

## 🌿 First Reading 🌿

**Acts 14:21** After they had proclaimed the good news to that city and had made many disciples, they returned to Lystra, then on to Iconium and Antioch. ²² There they strengthened the souls of the disciples and encouraged them to continue in the faith, saying, 'It is through many persecutions that we must enter the kingdom of God.' [23] And after they had appointed elders for them in each church, with prayer and fasting they entrusted them to the Lord in whom they had come to believe.

[24] Then they passed through Pisidia and came to Pamphylia. [25] When they had spoken the word in Perga, they went down to Attalia. [26] From there they sailed back to Antioch, where they had been commended to the grace of God for the work that they had completed. [27] When they arrived, they called the church together and related all that God had done with them, and how he had opened a door of faith for the Gentiles.

## Initial observations

Last Sunday, we heard the start of this First Missionary Journey (only in Acts). Today we hear the conclusion of that gospel outreach in a somewhat hectic concatenation of places and people. In our time, the energy and apparent success may sound enviable.

## Kind of writing

The excerpt combines two literary phenomena familiar from the Acts: summary statements and travelogues.

## Origin of the reading

The First Missionary Journey is recounted in Acts 13:1–14:38. Many places and people are covered, but in reality four large scenes form the substance of the tale. (1) Salamis: 13:4–12; (2) Antioch in Pisidia: 13:14–53; (3) Iconium: 14:1–7 and (4) Lystra: 14:8–20a.

## Related Passages

Antioch was a very important centre in early Christianity. In its day, it was the third largest city (c. 300k inhabitants) in the Roman

Empire, after Rome (1m) and Alexandria (500k) in Egypt. A large Jewish population made it a centre of faith and scholarship, as we know from the Talmud and Josephus, but also the *Chronographia* of Malalas.

No fewer than sixteen cities named Antioch were founded by Seleucus I Nicator. Two are important for early Christianity: Antioch in (or near) Pisidia and Antioch in Syria (Antioch-on-the-Orontes). Somewhat confusingly, both of these are named in our reading today.

## Brief commentary

### (V. 21)
Derbe is meant. Nothing is known of what happened in Derbe and even the site itself has not been excavated. This Antioch is in Pisidia.

### (V. 22)
'Strengthening' is a typical activity of the Apostles. Cf. Acts 15:41 (Syria and Cilicia); 18:43 (Galatia and Phrygia); 16:5 (general summary). Another word used in the same context is 'encouraging', which links the Pauline and Petrine missions. The content is given in brief form in v. 22: persecutions are the path of entry to the kingdom. Cf. Acts 9:16.

### (V. 23)
Elders as a term for church leaders first occurs in Acts 11:30. Prayer (Acts 1:14, 24; 2:42; 3:1; 4:31; 6:4, 6; 7:59; 8:15, 22, 24; 9:11, 40; 10:2, 4, 9, 30–31; 11:5; 12:5, 12; 13:3; 14:23; 16:13, 16, 25; 20:36; 21:5; 22:17; 26:29; 27:29; 28:8) and fasting (Acts 13:2–3; 14:23; 27:9) are featured frequently in Acts.

### (V. 24)
Pisidia was a small administrative unit and its capital was Antioch. Paul turned to the Gentiles in Pisidia (Acts 13:46). Phrygia was an ethnic territory in the eastern part of the Roman province of Asia.

### (V. 25)
Perga was an important city in Pamphylia. In the Acts, it is there that John, Mark and Paul parted company (Acts 13:13–14).

(V. 26)

Attalia was a port city (modern Antalya), founded by and named after Attalus II Philadelphus of Pergamon (159–138 BC).

(V. 27)

The work they completed was proclaiming the good news, making disciples, strengthening, exhorting and preparing for suffering. The original mandating runs: Now in the church at Antioch there were prophets and teachers: Barnabas, Simeon who was called Niger, Lucius of Cyrene, Manaen a member of the court of Herod the ruler, and Saul. While they were worshipping the Lord and fasting, the Holy Spirit said, 'Set apart for me Barnabas and Saul for the work to which I have called them.' Then after fasting and praying they laid their hands on them and sent them off (Acts 13:1–3).

Luke makes it explicit that it was not the achievement of the apostles but rather all that God had done with them. Cf. Acts 15:4, 12. The door of faith is an unusual expression, but it does occur in Paul: But I will stay in Ephesus until Pentecost, for a *wide door* for effective work has opened to me, and there are many adversaries (1 Corinthians 16:8–9); When I came to Troas to proclaim the good news of Christ, a *door* was opened for me in the Lord; but my mind could not rest because I did not find my brother Titus there. So I said farewell to them and went on to Macedonia (2 Corinthians 2:12–13). There is even an echo in the Deutero–Pauline Letters: 'At the same time pray for us as well that God will open to us a *door for the word*, that we may declare the mystery of Christ, for which I am in prison, so that I may reveal it clearly, as I should' (Colossians 4:3–4).

## Pointers for prayer

a) What is my own source of energy for evangelisation? Is there a community of faith 'behind' me?

b) Where do I see the open door of faith today, in spite of difficulties?

## Prayer

*God of the good news of salvation, you entrust us with the word of life. As we meet indifference and opposition, open the door of faith for all in need of your love and compassion. Show us how we can be true apostles not only in word but also in deed, so that many may be drawn to the beauty of the Gospel vision. We ask this through Jesus your Son, who lives and reigns with you in the unity of the Holy Spirit, God for ever and ever. Amen.*

## Themes across the readings

The first and third readings are not particularly linked, as often happens in the lectionary in Eastertide. Perhaps the very last line of the gospel hints at a connection: 'By this love you have for one another, everyone will know that you are my disciples.' Psalm 145 (144) takes up the theme of evangelising: *They shall speak of the glory of your reign and declare your might, O God, to make known to men your mighty deeds and the glorious splendour of your reign.*

# Chapter 6

## Easter 6C

## Thought for the day

There is a move afoot to replace Church teaching on the just war with a more proactive doctrine of just peace. As Paul VI observed long ago, peace is much more than the absence of war. In a world riven by conflict, peace is a matter of discipleship and, at the personal level, a matter of deliberate choice even in the everyday conflicts of our ordinary lives. The prayer for peace goes well beyond praying for individualistic freedom from stress.

## Prayer

*O God, though the human race is divided by dissension and discord, yet we know that by testing us you change our hearts to prepare them for reconciliation. Even more, by your Spirit you move human hearts that enemies may speak to each other again, adversaries may join hands, and peoples seek to meet together. Through Christ our Lord. Amen.*

## 🌿 Gospel 🌿

**Jn 14:22** Judas (not Iscariot) said to Jesus, 'Lord, how is it that you will reveal yourself to us, and not to the world?' 23 Jesus answered him, 'Those who love me will keep my word, and my Father will love them, and we will come to them and make our home with them. 24 Whoever does not love me does not keep my words; and the word that you hear is not mine, but is from the Father who sent me.

[25] 'I have said these things to you while I am still with you. [26] But the Advocate, the Holy Spirit, whom the Father will send in my name, will teach you everything, and remind you of all that I have said to you. [27] Peace I leave with you; my peace I give to you. I do not give to you as the world gives. Do not let your hearts be troubled, and do not let them be afraid. [28] You heard me say to you, "I am going away, and I am coming to you." If you loved me, you would rejoice that I am going to the Father, because the Father is greater than I. [29] And now I have told you this before it occurs, so that when it does occur, you may believe.'

## Initial observations

This is part of a longer speech in John 14–17, where Jesus prepares his disciples for his absence. It takes place at the Last Supper and corresponds in the Fourth Gospel to the shorter speeches at the Lord's Supper in the other three gospels. The opening verse has been added to give the context.

## Kind of writing

This belongs to the literary category of Farewell Discourse. The common situation in almost all of these instances is that of a prominent person who gathers his followers (children, disciples or the entire nation of Israel) just before his death or departure to give them final instructions, which will help them after he is gone. In our passage, Jesus prepares the disciples for this absence (i) by the commandment of love; (ii) by the promise of the Advocate, the Holy Spirit; (iii) by the gift of peace; (iv) by an invitation to rejoice that he departs; (v) by informing them beforehand. As usual in the Fourth Gospel, we are not dealing with a transcript, but with a profound meditation on Christian life in the period after the resurrection, placed on the lips of Jesus by the author. These are really the present gifts of the Risen Lord, present in the community.

## Old Testament background

(i) In the Old Testament, God's Holy Spirit is present in creation, inspires prophets and imparts the gift of Wisdom. This gospel adds to these functions the roles of 'advocacy' (paraclete = advocate) and 'reminding.'

(ii) Peace or *shalom* enjoys a high profile in the Old Testament with a distinctive range of meanings: physical well-being, fertility in family and crops, good relations with others. See Psalm 122.

(iii) One of the most common phrases across the whole Bible is 'Do not be afraid'. This is said to everyone who has an encounter with the transcendent. The Johannine form of this is 'Do not let your hearts be troubled, and do not let them be afraid.' Cf. Genesis 15:1; 21:17; 26:24; 35:17; 43:23; 46:3; 50:19; Exodus 14:13; 20:20; Numbers 21:34; Deuteronomy 7:18; Joshua 10:25; 11:6; Ruth 3:11; 1 Samuel 4:20; 12:20; 22:23; 23:17; 2 Samuel 9:7; 13:28; 1 Kings 17:13; 2 Kings 1:15; 6:16; 19:6; 25:24; 1 Chronicles 22:13; 28:20; 2 Chronicles 32:7; Nehemiah 4:14; Psalm 49:16; Proverbs 3:25; Isaiah 10:24; 37:6; 41:10; Jeremiah 1:8; 10:5; 40:9; 42:11; Ezekiel 2:6; Zechariah 8:13, 15; Tobit 4:8, 21; 6:18; 12:17; Judith 11:1; 1 Maccabees 3:22; 2 Esdras 6:33; 10:55; Matthew 1:20; 10:31; 14:27; 17:7; 28:5, 10; Mark 6:50; Luke 1:13, 30; 2:10; 5:10; 12:7, 32; John 6:20; 12:15; Acts 18:9; 27:24; Revelation 1:17. (Excuse the completeness of the references, but it does serve to make the point!)

## New Testament foreground

Then Jesus said to the Jews who had believed in him, 'If you continue in my word, you are truly my disciples (John 8:31). Why do you not understand what I say? It is because you cannot accept my word (John 8:43). Very truly, I tell you, whoever keeps my word will never see death' (John 8:51). Though you do not know him. But I know him; if I would say that I do not know him, I would be a liar like you. But I do know him and I keep his word (John 8:55). I do not judge anyone who hears my words and does not keep them, for I came not to judge the world, but to save the world (John 12:47). If you abide in me, and my words abide in you, ask for whatever you wish, and it will be done for you (John 15:7). Remember the word that I said to you, 'Servants are not greater than their master.' If they persecuted me, they will persecute you; if they kept my word, they will keep yours also (John 20). 'I have made your name known to those whom you gave me from the world. They were yours, and you gave them to me, and they have kept your word (John 17:6).

*The word that you hear is not mine*
John 14:10; 5:19–23, 30; 6:38; 7:16–18; 8:15–16, 28–29, 38; 12:49; 15:15; 17:7–8

*The advocate will teach you everything*
John 14:16, 26; 15:26; 16:7, 12–15

*Peace*
John 16:33; 20:19–26

*The Father is greater than I*
John 1:1–2, 12; 10:30, 38; 14:9–10; 20:17; 20:28

## St Paul

Therefore, since we are justified by faith, we have peace with God through our Lord Jesus Christ, through whom we have obtained access to this grace in which we stand; and we boast in our hope of sharing the glory of God. And not only that, but we also boast in our sufferings, knowing that suffering produces endurance, and endurance produces character, and character produces hope, and hope does not disappoint us, because God's love has been poured into our hearts through the Holy Spirit that has been given to us. (Romans 5:1–5)

For the kingdom of God is not food and drink but righteousness and peace and joy in the Holy Spirit. The one who thus serves Christ is acceptable to God and has human approval. Let us then pursue what makes for peace and for mutual upbuilding. (Romans 14:17–19)

Rejoice in the Lord always; again I will say, Rejoice. Let your gentleness be known to everyone. The Lord is near. Do not worry about anything, but in everything by prayer and supplication with thanksgiving let your requests be made known to God. And the peace of God, which surpasses all understanding, will guard your hearts and your minds in Christ Jesus. (Philippians 4:4–7)

## Brief commentary

(V. 23)
Home here could be rendered 'abode', corresponding to the verb 'abide'. In the words of the Fourth Gospel, Jesus is outlining the mutuality of indwelling which will mark the post-resurrection period. 'If you love me, you will keep my commandments' (John 14:15). 'If you keep my commandments, you will abide in my love, just as I have kept my Father's commandments and abide in his love' (John 15:10).

(V. 24)
The mutuality is available only for those who are obedient to the love commandment. Jesus mediates the word of the Father: 'I can do nothing on my own. As I hear, I judge; and my judgment is just, because I seek to do not my own will but the will of him who sent me' (John 5:30). 'Then Jesus cried out as he was teaching in the temple, "You know me, and you know where I am from. I have not come on my own. But the one who sent me is true, and you do not know him"'(John 7:28).

(V. 25)
The tone is that of 'farewell discourse' and the time is short. 'In a little while the world will no longer see me, but you will see me; because I live, you also will live' (John 14:19). Cf. 16:16–19.

**(V. 26)**

Remembering and understanding later are part of the theology of the Fourth Gospel. Only in the light of the resurrection and by the power of the Holy Spirit (unique here in the New Testament) can true insight into Jesus' ministry and identity be reached. See for example 2:22 or 20:9. On the Holy Spirit, see 14:15–17.

**(V. 27)**

The special peace of the risen Lord is freedom from death and from the fear of death. See 14:1–7. In the biblical view, true peace – *shalom* – is enjoyed by those in continuing relationship with God.

**(V. 28)**

The going points to death and resurrection – the ground of Christian joy (and peace). This gospel teaches the equality of the Father and the Son and at the same time the priority of the Father (as the parent-child metaphor suggests). The Son obeys the Father (heretics exploited this verse!). His 'going away' is for their benefit.

**(V. 29)**

In this gospel everything is done so that we may believe. See John 20:30–31.

## Pointers for prayer

a) Jesus seeks to reassure his followers in the face of his imminent death. Although he will be leaving them he promises them the gift of the Spirit. How have you been aware of the gift of the Spirit of God in your life?

b) Remember times of separation from a loved one through change of residence or other circumstances. How has the love between you been a support after the separation?

c) To his followers Jesus promises 'we will come and make our home with them'. Our God is not a distant God but one who lives in us. What has helped you to be aware of the closeness of God to you?

d) 'Do not let your hearts be troubled or afraid.' When you have been anxious, who have been the Jesus people for you who were able to calm your anxiety? How did they do this? For whom have you been one who calmed anxiety?

## Prayer

*Great and loving Father, your will for us in Jesus is the peace the world cannot give; your abiding gift is the Advocate he promised. Calm all troubled hearts, dispel every fear. Keep us steadfast in love and faithful to your word, that we may always be your dwelling place. Grant this through Jesus Christ, the first-born from the dead, who lives with you in the unity of the Holy Spirit, God for ever and ever. Amen.*

## 🌿 Second Reading 🌿

**Rev 21:9** *Then one of the seven angels who had the seven bowls full of the seven last plagues came and said to me, 'Come, I will show you the bride, the wife of the Lamb.'* [10] And in the spirit he carried me away to a great, high mountain and showed me the holy city Jerusalem coming down out of heaven from God. [11] It has the glory of God and a radiance like a very rare jewel, like jasper, clear as crystal. [12] It has a great, high wall with twelve gates, and at the gates twelve angels, and on the gates are inscribed the names of the twelve tribes of the Israelites; [13] on the east three gates, on the north three gates, on the south three gates, and on the west three gates. [14] And the wall of the city has twelve foundations, and on them are the twelve names of the twelve apostles of the Lamb.

[15] *The angel who talked to me had a measuring rod of gold to measure the city and its gates and walls.* [16] *The city lies foursquare, its length the same as its width; and he measured the city with his rod, fifteen hundred miles; its length and width and height are equal.* [17] *He also measured its wall, one hundred forty-four*

*cubits by human measurement, which the angel was using.* [18]
*The wall is built of jasper, while the city is pure gold, clear as
glass.* [19] *The foundations of the wall of the city are adorned with
every jewel; the first was jasper, the second sapphire, the third
agate, the fourth emerald,* [20] *the fifth onyx, the sixth carnelian,
the seventh chrysolite, the eighth beryl, the ninth topaz, the tenth
chrysoprase, the eleventh jacinth, the twelfth amethyst.* [21] *And
the twelve gates are twelve pearls, each of the gates is a single
pearl, and the street of the city is pure gold, transparent as glass.*

[22] I saw no temple in the city, for its temple is the Lord God
the Almighty and the Lamb. [23] And the city has no need of
sun or moon to shine on it, for the glory of God is its light,
and its lamp is the Lamb.

## Initial observations

Our reading from the Apocalypse brings it to a resounding close with
this tremendous vision, before concluding with prophetic sayings and
the epistolary ending. The Apocalypse can be impenetrable, but this
passage should speak easily enough.

## Kind of writing

Chapter 3 has the full outline of the book of Revelation. Our reading
comes from the last major section, Revelation 21:9–22:5. It comes as a
relief, after all the wars, destruction, upheaval and violence of the book.
Properly, it begins with v. 9, included here, as are vv. 15–21. It is obvious
why these verses were omitted but they do help us to understand the
reading better.

## Origin of the reading

The context is, as always, that of persecution or harassment on account
of being believers. The writer has in mind always the destruction of the
Temple in Jerusalem. There is no need of a temple, a distinct 'location'

for God's presence, because God will be all in all (1 Corinthians 15:28). The writer also has in mind the destruction of the great Babylon (i.e. Rome) and its replacement by another city, the new Jerusalem.

## Related passages

> And the one seated there looks like jasper and carnelian, and around the throne is a rainbow that looks like an emerald. (Revelation 4:3)

## Brief commentary

**(V. 9)**
V. 9 maintains the links with the previous upheavals. This angel was mentioned earlier in 15:1 (one of the seven bowls) and comes here to show the seer the bride of the Lamb (see 19:7). The bride contrasts with the whore in Revelation 17:3.

**(V. 10)**
This 'removal' of the seer parallels an earlier removal to view another city, Babylon-Rome (17:3). The high mountain is an echo of Ezekiel.

**(V. 11)**
Ezekiel is in mind here: Ezekiel 43:4. The jewellery contrasts sharply with the decorations of Babylon in Revelation 17:4, 18:12, 16. Cf. ' ... and they saw the God of Israel. Under his feet there was something like a pavement of sapphire stone, like the very heaven for clearness' (Exodus 24:10).

**(Vv. 12–13)**
A clear reference to a passage in Exodus: 'There shall be twelve stones with names corresponding to the names of the sons of Israel; they shall be like signets, each engraved with its name, for the twelve tribes' (Exodus 28:21). Cf. Ezekiel 48:30ff. and Ephesians 2:20.

**(V. 14)**
Curiously, this is the only explicit mention of the apostles in the Apocalypse. Notice that the twelve tribes and the twelve apostles are

both represented, thus uniting in symbolic fashion God's first and second chosen peoples.

**(Vv. 15–21)**

See Ezekiel 48:8–35 for the full background. 'A row of carnelian, chrysolite and emerald shall be the first row; and the second row a turquoise, a sapphire and a moonstone; and the third row a jacinth, an agate, and an amethyst; and the fourth row a beryl, an onyx and a jasper; they shall be set in gold filigree' (Exodus 28:17–20).

**(V. 22)**

Confining God to one people and one place is not part of the vision: God and the Lamb are present fully, everywhere, always and to everyone. God's presence constitutes the Temple, which is the whole world. Cf. John 4:23–24.

**(V. 23)**

This contrasts sharply withs the darkness of Babylon-Rome in Revelation 16:10 and 18:23. For light in the Apocalypse, see Revelation 8:12; 18:1, 23; 21:23–24; 22:5.

## Pointers for prayer

a) The light offers a (future) vision to sustain the persecuted in the present. What 'vision' sustains me?

b) Make your own list of the foundation stones and gates that are part of your spiritual life.

c) Light: such a beautiful phenomenon, directing our hearts to God.

## Prayer

*God of light, ever present to us all, shine once more into the darkness of our lives. Let your Holy Spirit radiate hope and trust into our hearts, that we too may know your light and bring it to others. Amen.*

## 🌿 First Reading 🌿

**Acts 15:1** Then certain individuals came down from Judea and were teaching the brothers, 'Unless you are circumcised according to the custom of Moses, you cannot be saved.' [2] And after Paul and Barnabas had no small dissension and debate with them, Paul and Barnabas and some of the others were appointed to go up to Jerusalem to discuss this question with the apostles and the elders.

[22] Then the apostles and the elders, with the consent of the whole church, decided to choose men from among their members and to send them to Antioch with Paul and Barnabas. They sent Judas called Barsabbas, and Silas, leaders among the brothers, [23] with the following letter: 'The brothers, both the apostles and the elders, to the believers of Gentile origin in Antioch and Syria and Cilicia, greetings. [24] Since we have heard that certain persons who have gone out from us, though with no instructions from us, have said things to disturb you and have unsettled your minds, [25] we have decided unanimously to choose representatives and send them to you, along with our beloved Barnabas and Paul, [26] who have risked their lives for the sake of our Lord Jesus Christ. [27] We have therefore sent Judas and Silas, who themselves will tell you the same things by word of mouth. [28] For it has seemed good to the Holy Spirit and to us to impose on you no further burden than these essentials: [29] that you abstain from what has been sacrificed to idols and from blood and from what is strangled and from fornication. If you keep yourselves from these, you will do well. Farewell.'

## Initial observations

A key issue in early Christianity was how much of the Jewish Law should be retained and how much set aside. It exercised many figures and writers: Paul, Peter and James, for instance. It wasn't just a question of legalism (our issue?) but rather of identity. And behind the question of identity lay another question: was the Gospel really for all or just for one race and converts to it? Paul would take it even deeper – behind the question stands an understanding of the cross: 'I do not nullify the grace of God; for if justification comes through the law, then Christ died for nothing' (Galatians 2:21). 'Listen! I, Paul, am telling you that if you let yourselves be circumcised, Christ will be of no benefit to you' (Galatians 5:2).

## Kind of writing

Most of the reading is made up of a letter and from it we can learn a great deal. It follows the usual format of a letter, which is a bit different from ours. For instance, the sender is mentioned first. Also, because there was no public postal system (there was an imperial one, however), letters were borne by members of the community. These were not simply bearers, but had the job of explaining the content by word of mouth, as indicated here.

## Origin of the reading

Our story is the so-called council of Jerusalem. An earlier gathering is reported in Acts 11:1–18. Luke tends to airbrush out the very real tensions and a quite different picture emerges from Paul's own account of the same encounter in Galatians. The New Testament quotations below attempt to capture the robustness of the exchanges and the urgency of the issue!

## Related passages

Various versions of other key moments may be found here: Acts 11:1–18 (the 'first' council of Jerusalem); 10:9–16 (Peter's threefold dream) and Galatians 2:11–14 (Paul's earlier account of what transpired, from the hand of a participant).

But when Cephas came to Antioch, I opposed him to his face, because he had clearly done wrong. Until certain people came from James, he had been eating with the Gentiles. But when they arrived, he stopped doing this and separated himself because he was afraid of those who were pro-circumcision. And the rest of the Jews also joined with him in this hypocrisy, so that even Barnabas was led astray with them by their hypocrisy. But when I saw that they were not behaving consistently with the truth of the gospel, I said to Cephas in front of them all, 'If you, although you are a Jew, live like a Gentile and not like a Jew, how can you try to force the Gentiles to live like Jews?' (Galatians 2:11–14)

## Brief commentary

(V. 1)
This first scene (in Syria) takes place in Antioch. Jews from Judea are Christ-believing Jews, claiming a special authority.

(V. 2)
It was a major issue, so a conference is set up to deal with it. At this point in Acts 15 both Peter and James make speeches, omitted in the lectionary, and we jump to the decision and the resultant communication.

(V. 22)
A substantial embassy is set up to convey the Jerusalem decision to the church in Antioch, underlining the importance of the event.

(V. 23)
The letter opening makes the addressees clear: believers of Gentile origin. The message is to them and through them to all.

(V. 24)
A needed preamble, detaching the senders from the 'persons who have gone out from us'. How they felt about being undermined is not recorded!

(V. 25)

Unanimity, in the Acts, is a sign that the Spirit is in charge. Thus the embassy enjoys the authority of the conference. Both sides, so to speak, are part of the embassy.

(V. 26)

The reputation of the apostles is affirmed. Probably the Gentiles did not need this apostolic affirmation but it is good to have it from the Jerusalem apostles.

(V. 27)

Silas and Judas bear the letter and also have the task of explaining it. This is the standard procedure with the New Testament letters as a whole.

(V. 28)

The sequence is important: first to the Holy Spirit and only then to us. That order has not always been evident! The message is fundamentally pastoral: let's not make things harder for those who want to join us.

(V. 29)

Food sacrificed to idols remained an issue as we learn from 1 Corinthians 8 and Romans 14. The risk was seeming to be in communion with idols. In the biblical tradition, the life is in the blood and so blood is forbidden, as in non-kosher meat ('strangled'). So, some of the food laws remain but circumcision is not insisted upon. In other words, the final decision was a compromise, in some contrast with the clarity of Paul in Galatians and Romans. Lest we think compromise a bad thing, it is at the service of the minimal conditions for communion and common life between Christians of Jewish and Gentile backgrounds. A not dissimilar discernment is offered in Romans 14. In the context, the mention of fornication may not be a reference to sexual sin but rather to false worship, as frequently in the Old Testament. Thus, all three prohibitions are focused on the one issue.

## Pointers for prayer

a) Conflict is normal within the community of faith. What is different is how we resolve conflict.

b) The desire not to make things difficult for those who wish to join us reflects the teaching of Jesus: 'But Jesus replied, "Woe to you experts in religious law as well! You load people down with burdens difficult to bear, yet you yourselves refuse to touch the burdens with even one of your fingers!"' (Luke 11:46). How do I welcome people to the community of faith?

c) Acting in communion with others is laborious but is really the only way. What has my experience taught me?

## Prayer

*O God of freedom: teach us how to be truly free that we may not lay burdens on ourselves and fellow believers. O God of welcome: show us how to welcome those who wish to walk with us in faith in a spirit of love and service. We make our prayer through our Lord Jesus Christ, your Son, who lives and reigns with you in the unity of the Holy Spirit, God for ever and ever. Amen.*

## Themes across the readings

Although not especially linked, a certain pattern can be detected in today's first and third readings. The issues which arose in the Council of Jerusalem triggered a huge discernment, highly significant for the evolution of Christianity. We believe that in the process of discernment, we are not alone because the Holy Spirit will teach us everything. Given the issue at stake in Acts, Psalm 67 makes a perfectly fitting response:

Let the peoples praise you, O God;
    let all the peoples praise you.
May God still give us his blessing
    till the ends of the earth revere him.

# Chapter 7

## Ascension C

## Thought for the day

As the Easter season draws to a close, both the liturgy and the lectionary point us towards the clothing with power from on high. In these days, our prayer is 'Come, Holy Spirit'. Each year, this prayer is of greater urgency, as we all try to listen to what the Spirit is saying to the churches. Our future being as Christians, as community, as church, depends on our own deep attitude of listening and of openness. The future Church will be a church of the Spirit, energised and exuberant, faithful and on fire.

## Prayer

*Breathe into me, Holy Spirit, that my thoughts may all be holy. Move in me, Holy Spirit, that my work, too, may be holy. Attract my heart, Holy Spirit, that I may love only what is holy. Strengthen me, Holy Spirit, that I may defend all that is holy.*

*Protect me, Holy Spirit, that I may always be holy. Glory be to the Father, and to the Son and to the Holy Spirit. Amen.*

## 🌿 Gospel 🌿

**Lk 24:36** *While they were talking about this, Jesus himself stood among them and said to them, 'Peace be with you.'* [37] *They were startled and terrified, and thought that they were seeing a ghost.* [38] *He said to them, 'Why are you frightened, and why do doubts arise in your hearts?* [39] *Look at my hands and my feet; see that it is I myself. Touch me and see; for a ghost does not have flesh* *and bones as you see that I have.'* [40] *And when he had said this, he showed them his hands and his feet.* [41] *While in their joy they were disbelieving and still wondering, he said to them, 'Have you anything here to eat?'* [42] *They gave him a piece of broiled fish,* [43] *and he took it and ate in their presence.*

[44] *Then he said to them, 'These are my words that I spoke to you while I was still with you—that everything written about me in the law of Moses, the prophets, and the psalms must be fulfilled.'* [45] *Then he opened their minds to understand the scriptures,* [46] and he said to them, 'Thus it is written, that the Messiah is to suffer and to rise from the dead on the third day, [47] and that repentance and forgiveness of sins is to be proclaimed in his name to all nations, beginning from Jerusalem. [48] You are witnesses of these things. [49] And see, I am sending upon you what my Father promised; so stay here in the city until you have been clothed with power from on high.'

[50] Then he led them out as far as Bethany, and, lifting up his hands, he blessed them. [51] While he was blessing them, he withdrew from them and was carried up into heaven. [52] And they worshipped him, and returned to Jerusalem with great joy; [53] and they were continually in the temple blessing God. While Jesus was blessing them, he withdrew from them

## Initial observations

The first couple of verses are not given in the lectionary, but as they seem essentially part of the scene they are included in italics. The endings of all the gospels are especially significant (even Mark 16:8, the original, disconcerting 'non-ending'). There is a special flavour to the ending in Luke because it bridges a two-volume work, synthesising comprehensively yet unobtrusively the themes of the Third Gospel and leaving the reader in a mood of anticipation. Chronologically, the readings today are the wrong way around – it would make more sense to hear this reading first and only then to move to the one from Acts.

## Kind of writing

This is the last scene in the gospel narrative, so it conforms to the functions of a peroration – to summarise, to engage the reader one final time, to intensify the emotional impact. The passage summarises both the ministry and the Lucan interpretation of it, by means of the typical themes and vocabulary of this gospel (words, written, fulfilled, open, Jerusalem, taken up). The potent vocabulary of the early Christian mission (messiah, suffer, rise, repentance, forgiveness, proclamation, witnesses) will speak directly to the intended readership. Finally, to the inherently emotional scene of separation ('while I was still with you'), the writer adds intense expectation ('until you have been clothed'), 'great joy' and the warm devotional atmosphere of Luke 1–2, evoked in the very last verse.

## Old Testament background

(i) By the time Luke was writing, Christians were accustomed to reading the Jesus story in the light of the First Testament. From our historical-critical point of view, they faced a huge task because the messiah, God's anointed and the agent of final salvation, is not mentioned as such in the Hebrew Bible. To grasp the expectation of the time, today we turn to the writings 'between the testaments', such as the Dead Sea Scrolls, the *Psalms of Solomon* and the *Testaments of the Twelve Patriarchs*. However, the first generation could find patterns like the Jesus story in prophets (especially in the Servant Songs of Isaiah) and in the Psalms (especially Psalm 2, 22 and 69). Hence, Luke can summarise by saying 'everything written about me'.

(ii) 'When they had crossed, Elijah said to Elisha, "Tell me what I may do for you, before I am taken from you." Elisha said, "Please let me inherit a double share of your spirit." He responded, "You have asked a hard thing; yet, if you see me as I am being taken from you, it will be granted you; if not, it

will not." As they continued walking and talking, a chariot of
fire and horses of fire separated the two of them, and Elijah
ascended in a whirlwind into heaven. Elisha kept watching
and crying out, "Father, father! The chariots of Israel and its
horsemen!" But when he could no longer see him, he grasped
his own clothes and tore them in two pieces. He picked up
the mantle of Elijah that had fallen from him, and went back
and stood on the bank of the Jordan. He took the mantle of
Elijah that had fallen from him, and struck the water, saying,
"Where is the Lord, the God of Elijah?" When he had
struck the water, the water was parted to the one side and to
the other, and Elisha went over.' (2 Kings 2:9–14)

## New Testament foreground

(i) The scene invites comparison with the closing moments
in Matthew 28:16–20 and John 20:30–31 (the original
ending). Continued presence and mission are the themes.

(ii) Within the Lucan narrative, the text reminds us of the
tableaux of Nazareth (Luke 4:16–30, 'Today this scripture
has been fulfilled in your hearing') and of the road to
Emmaus (Luke 24:13–35, 'Were not our hearts burning
within us while he was talking to us on the road, while he
was opening the scriptures to us?'), the two great theological
bookends of this gospel. In between, you have the 'passion
predictions' (Luke 9:22, 43–45; 18:31–34). The preaching in
Acts echoes the same theology of the suffering messiah.

(iii) There seems to be a 'pre-echo' of ascension itself, which
comes only after forty days in Acts 1:1–11.

(iv) The Holy Spirit, already the impulse behind Jesus' ministry,
becomes in the Acts the energy driving the expansion of the
Way from Jerusalem to Rome itself, from the heart of the
Jewish world to the heart of the Gentile one.

## St Paul

> Who is the one who will condemn? Is it Christ, the one who died (and more than that, he was raised), who is at the right hand of God, and who also is interceding for us? (Romans 8:34; New English Translation, adjusted)

## Brief commentary

### (V. 44)
God's word illuminates the ministry and person of Jesus. Notice the threefold contents: the Law (*Torah*), the prophets (*Nevi'im*) and the writings, (*Khethuvim*). Jews often refer to the Bible as the Tanakh, an acronym taken precisely from *Torah*, *Nevi'im* and *Khethuvim*.

### (V. 45)
A straight echo not only of Nazareth (Luke 4) and Emmaus (Luke 24), but also of the intriguing story of Philip and the eunuch (Acts 8:26–40, 'Do you understand what you are reading?').

### (V. 46)
Echoing the passion predictions and Emmaus, once more.

### (V. 47)
As usual, 'repentance' is better translated 'conversion'. Very important in Luke–Acts as a noun (Matthew [x2]; Mark [x1]; Luke [x5] and Acts [x6]) and as a verb (Matthew [x5]; Mark [x2]; Luke [x9] and Acts [x5]). The NRSV is wrong in talking about conversion and forgiveness. The Greek text speaks of conversion for forgiveness.

Proclamation (*kerygma*) occurs only here in the gospel, but the verb to proclaim is more common (x9 in Luke, and x8 in Acts). Jerusalem is symbolically important in Luke–Acts: the ministry moves towards the city and the mission sets out from it.

### (V. 48)
Witness (Greek, martyr) is important as noun (x2 in Luke; x13 in Acts) and as verb (x1 in Luke, x11 in Acts). See Acts 1:6–8, 22.

(V. 49)

The father's promise, an expression used again for the Holy Spirit in Acts 1:4–5, 8 and 2:4, 17–18, 38. 'Clothed' is not used again, but comes up in regard to Christ in Romans 13:12, 14; 1 Corinthians 15:53–54 and Galatians 5:27. 'From on high' takes us back to 'By the tender mercy of our God, the dawn from on high will break upon us' (Luke 1:78).

(V. 50)

Blessing is important in this gospel: Matthew (x5); Mark (x5); Luke (x13); John (x2). Bethany was the point from which Jesus planned his messianic entry into Jerusalem (19:29); he departs from the same location.

(V. 51)

The departing Lord leaves his blessing (and power) behind, just like the departing Elijah.

(V. 52)

Joy is the special mark of this gospel, both as a noun (Matthew [x6]; Mark x1]; Luke [x8]; Acts [x4]) and as a verb (Matthew [x6]; Mark [x2]; Luke [x12]; Acts [x7]). Great joy: Luke 2:10: But the angel said to them, 'Do not be afraid; for see – I am bringing you good news of great joy for all the people' (Acts 15:3). So they were sent on their way by the church, and as they passed through both Phoenicia and Samaria, they reported the conversion of the Gentiles, and brought *great joy* to all the believers.

(V. 53)

This is a direct echo of Zechariah and Simeon and Anna in Luke 1–2. The Temple remains a place of prayer for the disciples throughout the Acts, even though it had been destroyed by the time of writing.

## Pointers for prayer

a) The Ascension of Jesus was an important growth point for the disciples. Jesus would be with them in a different way from now on. Painful though it was, it was necessary for them to let go of his physical presence and adjust to the new reality. Perhaps you have known similar transition points in your own life.

b) Jesus invited the disciples to be witnesses to the good news they had learned. The way we live, speak and relate to others speaks of what we have learned about life. We all are witnesses. How have you been a witness to the goodness of life?

c) In particular, Jesus invited them to be witnesses to the good news of forgiveness. Recall people who have been witnesses to you of forgiveness and reconciliation. What effect did they have on your life? Have you been able to be a witness to the good news of forgiveness in your life?

d) In v. 49, Jesus instructs the apostles to wait patiently for the moment of grace. What has been your experience of waiting for a moment of grace? What are the moments of grace that you particularly recall (a friendship, a new opportunity, birth of a baby etc)?

## Prayer

*God of majesty, you led the messiah through suffering into risen life and took him up to the glory of heaven. Clothe us with the power promised from on high and send us forth to the ends of the earth as heralds of repentance and witnesses of Jesus Christ, the first-born from the dead, who lives and reigns with you in the unity of the Holy Spirit, God for ever and ever. Amen.*

## Second Reading

**Eph 1:15** I have heard of your faith in the Lord Jesus and your love toward all the saints, and for this reason [16] I do not cease to give thanks for you as I remember you in my prayers. [17] I pray that the God of our Lord Jesus Christ, the Father of glory, may give you a spirit of wisdom and revelation as you come to know him, [18] so that, with the eyes of your heart enlightened, you may know what is the hope to which he has called you, what are the riches of his glorious inheritance among the saints, [19] and what is the immeasurable greatness of his power for us who believe, according to the working of his great power. [20] God put this power to work in Christ when he raised him from the dead and seated him at his right hand in the heavenly places, [21] far above all rule and authority and power and dominion, and above every name that is named, not only in this age but also in the age to come. [22] And he has put all things under his feet and has made him the head over all things for the church, [23] which is his body, the fullness of him who fills all in all.

## Initial observations

The readers of every generation feature in this marvellous reflection and prayer. The sense of awe before the transcendent is palpable.

## Kind of writing

In the genuine letters from Paul, the letter format has been adjusted to include a longer thanksgiving for the faith of the recipients. In 2 Corinthians this takes the form of a 'blessing' prayer. In Ephesians, both styles are present.

vv. 3–14    Blessing prayer
vv. 15–23    Thanksgiving report

The introductory verses are included as usual in these books. In contrast to the genuine letters, there is no 'embedded' account of what is happening in the community. The other great prayer from Ephesians is offered below.

## Origin of the reading

It is not quite sure if this letter should be addressed to the Ephesians, because some important manuscripts lack the expression 'in Ephesus'. It has also proved difficult to establish the context in the community that occasioned the writing. (i) Is it to do with the famous and flourishing Artemis cult? (ii) It is to do with proto-gnostic mythologies? (iii) Or perhaps, some combination involving Jewish speculation on the heavenly journey? A clue is provided by the Dead Sea Scrolls, suggesting a Jew with a background in Jewish sectarianism. At the same time, the writing is very polished, so a Jew who enjoyed a good Hellenistic education (not unlike the apostle himself). Perhaps in a context of flourishing Judaism, the writer tries to bolster Christian identity. In any case, the vision is breathtaking, taking us well beyond the limits of the Roman Empire to a global expansion of the Gospel.

## Related Passages

> For this reason I bow my knees before the Father, from whom every family in heaven and on earth takes its name. I pray that, according to the riches of his glory, he may grant that you may be strengthened in your inner being with power through his Spirit, and that Christ may dwell in your hearts through faith, as you are being rooted and grounded in love. I pray that you may have the power to comprehend, with all the saints, what is the breadth and length and height and depth, and to know the love of Christ that surpasses knowledge, so that you may be filled with all the fullness of God. Now to him who by the power at work within us is able to accomplish abundantly far more than all we can ask or imagine, to him be glory in the church and in Christ Jesus to all generations, for ever and ever. Amen. (Ephesians 3:14–21)

## Brief commentary

(V. 17)
The writer moves from thanksgiving report to intercession. God's wisdom was already mentioned: In him we have redemption through his blood, the forgiveness of our trespasses, according to the riches of his

grace that he lavished on us. With all wisdom and insight he has made known to us the mystery of his will, according to his good pleasure that he set forth in Christ, as a plan for the fullness of time, to gather up all things in him, things in heaven and things on earth (Ephesians 1:7–10). The Spirit of wisdom probably ought to have a capital letter, pointing to a more than human wisdom.

(V. 18)

The language here is very close to that of the Essenes: 'May He enlighten your mind with wisdom for living, be gracious to you with the knowledge of eternal things, and lift up His gracious countenance upon you for everlasting peace' (1Qs 2:3–4). The eyes of your heart is unparalleled elsewhere but seems to suggest moral conduct. The content of that enlightenment is expanded in terms of Christian hope. Saints means simply fellow Christians, as opposed to angels or heavenly beings.

(V. 19)

The prayer turns to God at work in believers, the shift signalled by switching from 'you' to 'us'. What is this power?

(V. 20)

God's great deed is the resurrection of Jesus. Cf. Daniel 12:2–3; Acts 2:32–33; Philippians 2:9–11. Cf. also: 'In him also you were circumcised with a spiritual circumcision, by putting off the body of the flesh in the circumcision of Christ; when you were buried with him in baptism, you were also raised with him through faith in the power of God, who raised him from the dead' (Colossians 2:11–12).

(V. 21)

Being greater than heavenly powers comes up in Philippians 2:9–11 again and also in Hebrews 1:4–5.

(V. 22)

The expansion of the teaching in 1 Corinthians is evident: 'When all things are subjected to him, then the Son himself will also be subjected to the one who put all things in subjection under him, so that God may be all in all' (1 Corinthians 15:28).

(V. 23)

The mention of the church as body reminds us of Paul again in 1 Corinthians 12 and Romans 12. 'Fullness' does occur in the genuine Paul, usually in reference to the inclusion of the Gentiles. Here it is rather more cosmic: 'With all wisdom and insight he has made known to us the mystery of his will, according to his good pleasure that he set forth in Christ, as a plan for the fullness of time, to gather up all things in him, things in heaven and things on earth' (Ephesians 1:8–10).

## Pointers for prayer

a)  Recollect and reflect on my own moments of awe before God and the resurrection.

b)  What is my own sense of belonging and even inheritance?

## Prayer

*Mysterious God, nearer to us than we are to ourselves, we stand in silent awe before you and your deeds of power in the risen Christ. Through the same Christ, our Lord. Amen.*

## 🌿 First Reading 🌿

**Acts 1:1** In the first book, Theophilus, I wrote about all that Jesus did and taught from the beginning [2] until the day when he was taken up to heaven, after giving instructions through the Holy Spirit to the apostles whom he had chosen. [3] After his suffering he presented himself alive to them by many convincing proofs, appearing to them during forty days and speaking about the kingdom of God. [4] While staying with them, he ordered them not to leave Jerusalem, but to wait there for the promise of the Father. 'This,' he said, 'is what you have heard from me; [5] for John baptised with water, but you will be baptised with the Holy Spirit not many days from now.'

⁶ So when they had come together, they asked him, 'Lord, is this the time when you will restore the kingdom to Israel?' ⁷ He replied, 'It is not for you to know the times or periods that the Father has set by his own authority. ⁸ But you will receive power when the Holy Spirit has come upon you; and you will be my witnesses in Jerusalem, in all Judea and Samaria, and to the ends of the earth.'⁹ When he had said this, as they were watching, he was lifted up, and a cloud took him out of their sight. ¹⁰ While he was going and they were gazing up towards heaven, suddenly two men in white robes stood by them. ¹¹ They said, 'Men of Galilee, why do you stand looking up towards heaven? This Jesus, who has been taken up from you into heaven, will come in the same way as you saw him go into heaven.'

¹² *Then they returned to Jerusalem from the mount called Olivet, which is near Jerusalem, a sabbath day's journey away.* ¹³ *When they had entered the city, they went to the room upstairs where they were staying, Peter, and John, and James, and Andrew, Philip and Thomas, Bartholomew and Matthew, James son of Alphaeus, and Simon the Zealot, and Judas son of James.* ¹⁴ *All these were constantly devoting themselves to prayer, together with certain women, including Mary the mother of Jesus, as well as his brothers.*

## Initial observations

The Prologue to Luke's second volume is Acts 1:1–14 (the remaining three verses are added here to complete the genre). This elaborate introduction unfolds in four distinct moments. (1) A summary of the Gospel story (vv.1–3); (2) two representative scenes from the forty days of Easter fellowship between Jesus and the disciples (vv. 4–8); (3) the ascension proper (vv.9–11); (4) a summary statement to lead us in to the narrative of Acts (12–14). In effect, we have here a complex transition to the Acts, with many hints of what is to come.

## Kind of writing

This is both a prologue and a transition. A prologue should intrigue the reader/hearer by presenting the context (Jesus' definitive departure), the protagonists (the apostles, Mary), and the 'inciting moment', that is, suspense of the narrative (What will happen now that he is gone? The anticipated descent of the Holy Spirit). As a transition, the links with the gospel are clear (Theophilus), the new situation is named (the time after the forty days), the potential error of looking the wrong way is acknowledged, and a summary prepares us for the real beginning of the storytelling in Acts 1:15.

## Origin of the reading

The context is that of transition: How would the disciples 'manage' after the departure of Jesus?

## Related passages

> Since many have undertaken to set down an orderly account of the events that have been fulfilled among us, just as they were handed on to us by those who from the beginning were eyewitnesses and servants of the word, I too decided, after investigating everything carefully from the very first, to write an orderly account for you, most excellent Theophilus, so that you may know the truth concerning the things about which you have been instructed. (Luke 1:1–4)

> Then he led them out as far as Bethany, and, lifting up his hands, he blessed them. While he was blessing them, he withdrew from them and was carried up into heaven. And they worshipped him, and returned to Jerusalem with great joy; and they were continually in the temple blessing God. (Luke 24:50–53)

## Brief commentary

(V. 1)

The second volume begins with a summary of the Gospel, 'all that Jesus did and taught'. See Luke 4:16–30 for Luke's anticipatory synthesis.

(V. 2)

The ascension was already recounted in Luke 24:50–53 and the promise of the Holy Spirit is made in 24:49. A tremendous role is accorded to the Spirit in Acts, starting with the Pentecost scene. Cf. 'beginning' in Luke 1:2.

(V. 3)

Luke has in mind his own story of Jesus eating after the resurrection in Luke 24:36–43.

(V. 4)

The centrality of Jerusalem for the evangelist is clear. It is the historic city towards which Jesus turns his face (Luke 9:51), in which the events of salvation take place, and from which the 'word' will be brought to the whole world (symbolised by Rome). Cf. 'Being therefore exalted at the right hand of God, and having received from the Father the promise of the Holy Spirit, he has poured out this that you both see and hear' (Acts 2:33).

(V. 5)

The promised Spirit is given different names: clothed with power from on high (Luke 24:49); baptised with the Holy Spirit (Acts 2:1–12). Cf. Luke 3:16.

(V. 6)

The restoration of Israel was a key to Jesus' own ministry, as indicated by the choice of the Twelve, to symbolise the tribes, and by the apostles' desire to restore the number with the election of Matthias. The restoration of Israel was associated with the coming of the Spirit (cf. Ezekiel 37; Joel 2:28–32). The very same question of 'when' comes up elsewhere in the New Testament. Cf. Luke 1:35.

**(V. 7)**

Cf. a text from Mark omitted by Luke in his gospel: 'But about that day or hour no one knows, neither the angels in heaven, nor the Son, but only the Father' (Mark 13:32).

**(V. 8)**

After Pentecost, Jerusalem will lose its central role in God's purpose. Cf. universalist texts in Isaiah, such as Isaiah 8:9; 45:22; 48:20; 49:6; 62:10–11.

**(V. 9)**

The ascension metaphor echoes both exaltation and enthronement in power (see Psalm 110, frequently alluded to in the New Testament). There is a clear evocation of the departure of Elijah and the passing of the mantle to Elisha (here to the disciples).

**(V. 10)**

The two men specifically call to mind Luke's account of the empty tomb proclamation, where the two angels are first referred to as two men.

**(V. 11)**

In vv. 9–11, the emphasis on 'sight' (watching, sight, gazing, looking up, saw) prepares the apostles for their role as witnesses. Cf. Luke 21:27, and 24:5–6.

## Pointers for prayer

a) Significant transitions involved endings and beginnings. It may help to remember your own experience of this in ordinary life. Perhaps, too, there have been significant moments of 'before and after' in your discipleship?

b) In our culture, witnessing to the faith can invite dismissal, even ridicule. We can also meet welcome and encouragement. What has your experience been?

c) There is a palpable sense of anticipation in Acts 1:1–14. When have you waited on God, in prayer and in discernment? What did you learn? Prayer of openness to the Spirit.

# Prayer

*O God, giver of the Holy Spirit, we open our eyes to your vision, we open our hearts to your gift, we open our lives to your direction. We await your promise to be clothed in power from on high, so that we too may truly bring your good news in Christ to everyone in our time and to the ends of the earth. Through Christ our Lord. Amen.*

## Themes across the readings

The first reading and the gospel match each other closely. Respecting lectionary tradition, the Lucan chronological order (Luke–Acts) is inverted and we hear the later story first. In both readings, we witness the negotiation of continuity within discontinuity. Something is ending (the past ministry of Jesus) and something is beginning (the future mission of the church). Ephesians contributes to the understanding of church as the body of Christ. Psalm 47 (46) fits perfectly the feast and the readings: God goes up with shouts of joy; the Lord goes up with trumpet blast. The context of writing is most likely post-Exilic, when people had given up on earthly monarchs.

# Chapter 8

## Easter 7C

## Thought for the day

Sometimes the simpler, the deeper, and the deeper, the simpler. John's Gospel illustrates this: using no technical or esoteric vocabulary, the writer nevertheless manages to hold before us God, the 'beyond in the midst', in the happy phrase of Bonhoeffer.

In some senses, the deepest reality is also the simplest. *Love is our origin. Love is our constant calling. Love is our fulfilment in heaven.* None of the mystery is lost and yet none of the love is missed. The writer orientates us towards the Mystery, lost in wonder, love and praise.

## Prayer

*God, help us to recognise you, the divine beyond in the midst of the everyday reality. Spirit, inspire us to see the God of love in everyone and everything. Jesus, be with us always to the end of the age. To you be the glory, for ever and ever. Amen.*

## Gospel

**Jn 17:20** [Jesus said:] 'I ask not only on behalf of these, but also on behalf of those who will believe in me through their word, [21] that they may all be one. As you, Father, are in me and I am in you, may they also be in us, so that the world may believe that you have sent me. [22] The glory that you have given me I have given them, so that they may be one, as we are one,

²³ I in them and you in me, that they may become completely one, so that the world may know that you have sent me and have loved them even as you have loved me. ²⁴ Father, I desire that those also, whom you have given me, may be with me where I am, to see my glory, which you have given me because you loved me before the foundation of the world.

²⁵ 'Righteous Father, the world does not know you, but I know you; and these know that you have sent me. ²⁶ I made your name known to them, and I will make it known, so that the love with which you have loved me may be in them, and I in them.'

## Initial observations

John 17 is a kind of Cinderella chapter. The writer chose to bring Jesus' final discourse to a climax with these verses and yet they are read only on the seventh Sunday of Easter. Because so many places now celebrate the Ascension on that the Sunday, the chapter is almost never proclaimed on Sundays.

This a pity for the chapter as a whole but especially for these final few paragraphs. However, John 17 is read during the seventh week of Easter on Tuesday, Wednesday and Thursday, using the same divisions as in years A, B and C.

## Kind of writing

The whole of John 13–17 belongs to the genre of Farewell Discourse. The final chapter takes the following steps:

    i)  Jesus prays for his glorification and describes eternal life (1–5)
    ii)  The beginning of eternal life in the disciples (6–8)
    iii) Jesus prays for his disciples (9–19)
    iv) Jesus prays for future believers (20–24)
    v)  Jesus concludes his prayer (25–26)

The portions appointed for this Sunday are accordingly the final two units, vv. 20–26. All of John 17 is in some degree inspired by the Lord's Prayer.

| MATTHEW 6:9–13 | THE LORD'S PRAYER EMBEDDED IN JOHN 17 |
|---|---|
| Our Father | My father and your Father (John 20:17). Father! (John 11:41; 12:27-28; **17:1, 5, 11, 21, 24, 26**) |
| in heaven | Jesus looked up to heaven (John 11:41); Lifting his eyes to heaven (John **17:11**) |
| may your name be honoured | Glorify your name (John 12:28); My Father is honoured by this, that you bear much fruit and show that you are my disciples. (John 15:8) |
| may your kingdom come | Unless a person is born from above, he cannot see the kingdom of God. (John 3:3); Unless a person is born of water and spirit, he cannot enter the kingdom of God. (John 3:5) |
| may your will be done on earth as it is in heaven | For I have come down from heaven not to do my own will but the will of the one who sent me. (John 6:38) |
| Give us today our daily bread | Jesus said to them, 'My food is to do the will of the one who sent me and to complete his work. (John 4:34); my Father is giving you the true bread from heaven. (John 6:32); Sir, give us this bread all the time! (John 6:34) |
| and forgive us our debts | Look, the Lamb of God who takes away the sin of the world! (John 1:29) |
| as we ourselves have forgiven our debtors | 'I give you a new commandment – to love one another. Just as I have loved you, you also are to love one another. Everyone will know by this that you are my disciples – if you have love for one another.' (John 13:34-35) Cf. John 15:12, 17. |
| And do not lead us into temptation, but deliver us from the evil one | Keep them safe in your name that you have given me (John **17:11**); When I was with them I kept them safe and watched over them in your name that you have given me. (John **17:12**); I am not asking you to take them out of the world, but that you keep them safe from the evil one. (John **17:15**) |

## Old Testament background

> Declare and present your case; let them take counsel together! Who told this long ago? Who declared it of old? Was it not I, the LORD? There is no other god besides me, a *righteous God* and a Saviour; there is no one besides me. (Isaiah 45:21)

> O let the evil of the wicked come to an end, but establish the righteous, you who test the minds and hearts, O *righteous God*. (Psalm 7:9)

> For the LORD is righteous. (Psalm 11:7; 119:137; 129:4)

## New Testament foreground

> In the beginning was the Word, and the Word was with God, and the Word was God. (John 1:1)

> For God so loved the world that he gave his only Son, so that everyone who believes in him may not perish but may have eternal life. (John 3:16)

> Do not let your hearts be troubled. Believe in God, believe also in me. In my Father's house there are many dwelling places. If it were not so, would I have told you that I go to prepare a place for you? And if I go and prepare a place for you, I will come again and will take you to myself, so that where I am, there you may be also. And you know the way to the place where I am going.' Thomas said to him, 'Lord, we do not know where you are going. How can we know the way?' Jesus said to him, 'I am the way, and the truth, and the life. No one comes to the Father except through me. If you know me, you will know my Father also. From now on you do know him and have seen him. (John 14:1–7)

> They who have my commandments and keep them are those who love me; and those who love me will be loved by my Father, and I will love them and reveal myself to them. (John 14:21)

## St Paul

> Welcome one another, therefore, just as Christ has welcomed you, for the glory of God. For I tell you that Christ has become a servant of the circumcised on behalf of the truth of God in order that he might confirm the promises given to the patriarchs, and in order that the Gentiles might glorify God for his mercy. (Romans 15:7–9)

## Brief commentary

### (V. 20)

'Those who will believe' translates a present particle in Greek but the meaning is probably future, pointing to the increasingly Gentile reality of the Jesus movement. Their 'word' reflects a very early tradition meaning the Gospel *about* Jesus. See also John 4:39 and 20:29.

### (V. 21)

The insistence upon love and unity is quite revealing about the real state of things. The John community comprised quite diverse groups: followers of John the Baptist, Pharisees, Samaritans and Gentiles. As in any healthy community, there was conflict. Hence the intercession that they *may* all be one.

For 'as', the gospel uses the Greek adverb *kathōs*, which means far more than merely being inspired by or replicating the love of Jesus. In key places in this gospel, *kathōs* means that the sending, the serving, the loving, the self-giving of Jesus are continued immediately and directly in the sending, serving, loving and self-giving of true disciples. Our mission is literally his mission.

The desired unity is not a matter of compatibility or politics or compromise. On the contrary, the community draws its unity from the unity of the Father and the Son. This unity is not simply a desideratum, it also has an evangelical purpose: *that the world may believe*. See also John 17:8, 25.

(V. 22)

Glory, in this gospel, belongs to the category of revelation. Jesus was glorified in his death and resurrection, meaning that the very heart of God was disclosed through the lifting up. In this gospel, God *serves humanity* and reveals himself as lover to an astonishing, incredible degree. This 'glory' has been given to all believers, so that they too may continue to disclose God through their love, service and self-giving. The oneness of the community flows directly from their faith and their mission.

(V. 23)

The triple weave of this love is elusively hinted at: the threads can be distinguished (Father, Son and believers) but cannot be separated. Once again, this love has a purpose beyond the community: so that the world may know. The little word 'as' (*kathōs*) is used again, revealing the one love of the Father for the Son and for all who believe in him. The reader will not forget to recall John 3:16 at this point. See also 14:21, 23 and 16:27.

(V. 24)

In this gospel, the early Christian tension towards the end of time has been relaxed and scholars speak of realised eschatology (the present moment of salvation). But even so, there is a future, already made clear in John 14:1–7 (see above; 12:26; 14:3).

Again, glory points not to 'honour and glory' but to being and identity disclosed in Jesus. Behind it stands not the Greek concept of *doxa* (glory as appearance) but the Hebrew concept of *kŝloYa* (glory as substance, weight or importance). See John 17:5. The intricate 24c means that love, identity, disclosure and creation are all bound up together. Before the foundation of the world takes the reader back to the Prologue of the Gospel (see John 1:1 above) and the pre-existence of the Word.

(V. 25)

Various forms of 'to know' and 'to love' appear in prodigal fashion in these final verses. To know means more than to be acquainted with or to have information about. Instead, 'know' points to an interpersonal knowledge, the way Adam 'knew' his wife in Genesis 4:1, even though they had already been introduced! A loving knowledge is intended, a far deeper reality. On Jesus' lips 'I know you' can only mean 'I love you'. Even 25b cannot mean simply they have information – rather they have become wholeheartedly convinced of this reality with their entire being.

(V. 26)

Name points to the person, not simply a title. Jesus has disclosed the Father, and this disclosure is a disclosure of love. 'I will make it known' is a kind of future continuous: 'I will continue to make it known.'

## Pointers for prayer

a) Conflict is normal, but so is the desire for harmony and unity. How have I personally negotiated this tension as a person of faith and prayer?

b) Love should be our great calling card as Christians (as the song puts it: 'They will know we are Christians by our love.' Well, would they?).

c) Do I find myself moved and attracted by the visionary mysticism of John's Gospel – do I find myself drawn to it from deeply within myself?

## Prayer

*Father, righteous one, your beloved Son prayed that his disciples in every generation might be one as you and he are one. Look upon this assembly gathered in his name. Fulfil in us the prayer of Jesus and crown our celebration of this paschal season with your Spirit's gift of unity and love.*

*Grant this through Jesus Christ, the first-born from the dead, who lives and reigns with you in the unity of the Holy Spirit, God for ever and ever. Amen.*

# 🌿 Second Reading 🌿

**Rev 22:12** 'See, I am coming soon; my reward is with me, to repay according to everyone's work. [13] I am the Alpha and the Omega, the first and the last, the beginning and the end.'

[14] Blessed are those who wash their robes, so that they will have the right to the tree of life and may enter the city by the gates. [15] *Outside are the dogs and sorcerers and fornicators and murderers and idolaters, and everyone who loves and practises falsehood.*

[16] 'It is I, Jesus, who sent my angel to you with this testimony for the churches. I am the root and the descendant of David, the bright morning star.'

[17] The Spirit and the bride say, 'Come.'
And let everyone who hears say, 'Come.'
And let everyone who is thirsty come.
Let anyone who wishes take the water of life as a gift.

## Initial observations

Our exploration of the New Testament Apocalypse comes to a close today, with the closing blessings and invitations. After the cosmic struggle between good and evil, it is a relief to come to these final welcoming verses.

## Kind of writing

Our excerpt is part of the extended Epilogue and Benediction in 22:6b–21, combining several kinds of writing: a final affirmation by the risen Lord; a blessing and a curse (omitted in the lectionary), a further identification of Jesus followed by a wider invitation. These last few verses function as a *peroratio*, that is, a synthesis of summary, amplification and final appeal to the emotions. Readers of the time would not have been surprised to see these closing sentiments.

## Origin of the reading

Like all apocalyptic, the context is one of general harassment, even persecution, for faith. The concrete issue is emperor worship, deeply embedded socially and culturally and thus really hard to avoid. At this point, we are at the end of the book, and so final reassurances are given in a tone of invitation but also warning.

## Related passages

*Revelation is highly 'intertextual', as can be seen in these representative passages.*

> See, I am coming soon! Blessed is the one who keeps the words of the prophecy of this book. (Revelation 22:7)

> I am the first and the last, and the living one. I was dead, and see, I am alive forever and ever; and I have the keys of Death and of Hades. (Revelation 1:17–18)

> See, the Lion of the tribe of Judah, the Root of David, has conquered, so that he can open the scroll and its seven seals. (Revelation 5:5)

> A star shall come out of Jacob, and a sceptre shall rise out of Israel. (Numbers 24:17)

> These are they who have come out of the great ordeal; they have washed their robes and made them white in the blood of the Lamb. (Revelation 7:14)

> To everyone who conquers, I will give permission to eat from the tree of life that is in the paradise of God. (Revelation 2:7)

> To the one who conquers I will also give the morning star. (Revelation 2:28)

## Brief commentary

**(V. 12)**

It is Christ who is speaking here, affirming what the angel said in Revelation 22:7. Works, here, means witnessing to the Lordship of Jesus himself (2:2, 5, 6, 19, 23, 26; 3:1, 2, 8, 15). For the Last Judgment see Revelation 20:12–13.

**(V. 13)**

In an expression previously applied only to God (1:8; 21:6), Jesus now describes himself. Cf. Isaiah 44:6; 48.12. This is the highest identification of Jesus with God in the New Testament. He is now in charge of history.

**(V. 14)**

This is the seventh and final beatitude of the Apocalypse (1:3; 14:13; 16:15; 19:9; 20:6; 22:7, 14). Seven is not an accident and these beatitudes put before us what the writer really wanted his hearers to hear. The washing of robes takes us back to 7:14 and the blood of the Lamb. The tree of life, from Genesis, is referred to a few times: Revelation 2:7; 22:2, 14, 19. The city is the new Jerusalem, just described.

**(V. 15)**

This exclusionary curse reflects the binary world of the Apocalypse and serves as a warning. It is omitted in the lectionary excerpt, for pastoral reasons.

**(V. 16)**

The angel sent to the churches reminds us of the Letters to the Seven Churches in chs 2–3. The root of David, a symbol of fidelity, takes us back particularly to 5:5 and generally to the foundational liturgy in chs 4–5. The one who is the bright morning star also gives the gift of the bright morning star in Revelation 2:28. As noted earlier in the book, the revelation from God goes to Christ to the angel to the seer to the community.

(V. 17)

The Spirit of God now speaks (Revelation 2:7, 11, 17, 29; 3:6, 13, 22; 14:13) in a kind of liturgical responsory, picking up the worship setting of the whole book. The bride (Revelation 21:9–22:9) is the holy city, Jerusalem (in strong contrast to Rome) the whore of Babylon. Emperor worship was the ideology of the day and it took courage to resist. The invitation is then broadened to everyone – everyone who hears or thirsts or simply wishes to take the water of life. The nuptial imagery is an echo of the bridal imagery in John 2–4, where it is also paired with water as a symbol. The thirsty are not those on any 'spiritual journey' but those who specifically need and desire the eschatological relationship with Jesus. In brief, the ones who hear are the ones who conquer, because the 'hearers' are those who have heard, converted, obeyed and thus witnessed. Finally, it is all gift and grace!

*From the related passages and commentary, it is evident that these verses offer a summary, an amplification and an appeal to the emotions. Anyone who has got this far in the book or in its liturgical performance will not be unmoved.*

## Pointers for prayer

a) The reassurance of the Apocalypse is profound, a dramatised version of 'I will be with you always.' How have I needed such a message and in what circumstances?

b) Let the repeated invitation, 'come', resonate in your heart. Who is saying this to you at this point in your life?

c) We are all 'hearers of the word', called to conversion, obedience and faithful witness.

## Prayer

*Eternally faithful God, you have disclosed your faithfulness to us through the faithfulness of Jesus, your Son, the true witness. With the gift of the Spirit, stir up in each of us a desire to be faithful to you in everything, in all that we are and in all that we do. Through Christ our Lord. Amen.*

# 🍃 First Reading 🍃

**Acts 7:55** But filled with the Holy Spirit, Stephen gazed into heaven and saw the glory of God and Jesus standing at the right hand of God. [56] 'Look,' he said, 'I see the heavens opened and the Son of Man standing at the right hand of God!' [57] But they covered their ears, and with a loud shout all rushed together against him. [58] Then they dragged him out of the city and began to stone him; and the witnesses laid their coats at the feet of a young man named Saul. [59] While they were stoning Stephen, he prayed, 'Lord Jesus, receive my spirit.' [60] Then he knelt down and cried out in a loud voice, 'Lord, do not hold this sin against them.' When he had said this, he died *(ekoimēthē)*.

## Initial observations

Having arrived at Acts 15 last Sunday, we now go back to Acts 7, for the witness of Stephen. There are two keys for understanding this reading. (i) Stephen's witness (= *martyrion* in Greek) is inspired by the Spirit; (ii) the manner of Stephen's death purposefully echoes that of Jesus himself in Luke's Gospel. The example of costly witness comes before the feast of Pentecost, the gift of the Spirit who enables us to be witnesses.

## Kind of writing

The importance of the story of Stephen and his speech is clear because of the location and length of the story. It is part of a longer, somewhat concentric sequence in Acts 6:1–8:3, as follows:

1. The appointment of the Seven
2. The accusation against Stephen
3. The speech of Stephen
4. The death of Stephen
5. The persecution that followed

A.    Community and conflict
B.        Accusation
C.            Defence
B*.        *Killing*
A*.    Community and persecution

## Origin of the reading

Stephen, like Jesus in the Third Gospel, dies the death of an innocent martyr and thus takes his place as yet another example of a prophet who, because he spoke of 'the coming of the Righteous One' (Acts 7:52), is the victim of 'stiff-necked people,' who continue to persecute the representatives of God. It patterns the destiny of the true witness on Jesus' own destiny.

## Related passages

> As I watched in the night visions, I saw one like a like a Son of Man coming with the clouds of heaven. And he came to the Ancient One and was presented before him. (Daniel 7:13 NRSV adjusted)

> When they bring you before the synagogues, the rulers and the authorities, do not worry about how you are to defend yourselves or what you are to say; for the Holy Spirit will teach you at that very hour what you ought to say. (Luke 12:11–12)

> Jesus replied, 'If I tell you, you will not believe; and if I question you, you will not answer. But from now on the Son of Man will be seated at the right hand of the power of God.' (Luke 22:67–69)

> They got up, drove him out of the town, and led him to the brow of the hill on which their town was built, so that they might hurl him off the cliff. (Luke 4:29)

Then Jesus, crying with a loud voice, said, 'Father, into your hands I commend my spirit.' Having said this, he breathed his last (*exepneusen*). (Luke 23:46)

Then Jesus said, 'Father, forgive them; for they do not know what they are doing.' (Luke 23:34)

But Saul was ravaging the church by entering house after house; dragging off both men and women, he committed them to prison. (Acts 8:3)

## Brief commentary

(V. 55)
The scene is in Jerusalem, during the trial. Filled with the Spirit, Stephen has a vision of Jesus, a fulfilment of Luke 22:69. Standing *on the right* echoes Psalm 110:2 and Daniel 7:13. Jesus stands rather than sits (as in the psalm) because he is risen from the dead. The inspiration of the Spirit at this point is a fulfilment of Luke 12:11–12 above.

(V. 56)
Stephen reports the vision, because his accusers have not seen what he saw.

(V. 57)
The rush against Stephen echoes Luke 4:29, from the tableau of Luke 4:16–30, which prefigures the entire career of Jesus, including his death and resurrection.

(V. 58)
Taking him out of the city echoes Luke 4:29 once more and also anticipates Acts 13:50 and 16:37. Outside the city conforms to the rules for those who blaspheme in Leviticus 24:14 and Numbers 15:35–36. Saul is slipped in here for the first time, in a story that reflects his own account in 1 Corinthians 15:8, Galatians 1:13 and Philippians 3:6. The witnesses are the *martyres*, the literal meaning of the word, though an ironic reference to later Gospel witnesses cannot

be excluded. Our English word martyr originally meant witness and only later came to mean someone who bore witness *with their life*.

(V. 59)
Jesus prayed Psalm 31:5, a prayer of trust, to the Father, while Stephen entrusts himself to Jesus.

(V. 60)
The loud voice also echoes the death of Jesus in Luke. More importantly, the prayer for forgiveness obeys Jesus' teaching in Luke 6:37, as well as echoing his death in Luke 23:34 (a disputed text). There is a final point of contrast. When Jesus dies in Luke, it says literally he expired, meaning the breath or Spirit went out of him. In the case of Stephen, he falls asleep – the common metaphor for death in the culture, with a new depth of meaning because Jesus is the first fruits of all *who have fallen asleep*.

## Pointers for prayer

a)  The bearing of witness can be dramatic, as in the Stephen story, or more ordinary, as in our everyday experience. When have you felt the power of the Spirit, helping you to say the right words at the right time?

b)  Sometimes an experience or even the memory of it can give us courage when we need it. It does not have to be a 'vision' – any moment of presence or insight would do.

c)  Stephen ends his life with a great act of trust in Jesus, risen from the dead. Let us hope that we can do the same.

## Prayer

*God of every consolation and encouragement, in our day we are called to be witnesses to what we believe, to you yourself, to Jesus risen from the dead. Send us your Spirit so that we do not have to worry about what to say and when to say it but rather let the Spirit speak through us. Through Christ our Lord. Amen.*

## Themes across the readings

From the gospel and the second reading, we are invited to the deepest imaginable intimacy with God, nothing less. The language of the gospel is quite mystical – an invitation to oneness in and with the Mystery as such. The language of the Apocalypse is more evidently metaphorical, but no less inviting and invigorating. Stephen, too, is there, as he sees the heavens open!

Can we 'hear' this extraordinary invitation today? What would I need to put in place in my life that I may continue to hear the invitation and live it, as Stephen was able to do?

# Chapter 9

## Pentecost C

## Thought for the day

The four marks of our Christian belonging are our personal journey, our community belonging, our practical discipleship and our adult integration of faith and life. None of us 'inhabits' all four dimensions fully, all of the time, and yet all four dimensions should in principle be there. The good news of Pentecost is that the Spirit, poured into our hearts, enables all four aspects of our faith to live: the Spirit helps us in our prayer; the body of Christ is animated by the gifts of the Spirit; our service of others gets its energy from the Spirit and the Spirit 'reminds us' of all that Jesus taught. Today, we celebrate discipleship in the community of faith.

## Prayer

*We open our hearts and lives to you, Holy Spirit: breathe a breath of new life into us all! You live and reign in communion with the Father and Son, for ever and ever. Amen.*

## 🌾 Gospel 🌾

**Jn 20:19** When it was evening on that day, the first day of the week, and the doors of the house where the disciples had met were locked for fear of the Jews, Jesus came and stood among them and said, 'Peace be with you'. [20] After he said this, he showed them his hands and his side. Then the disciples rejoiced when they saw the Lord. [21] Jesus said to them again, 'Peace be with you. As the Father has sent me, so I send you.' [22] When he had said this, he breathed on them and said to them, 'Receive the Holy Spirit. [23] If you forgive the sins of any, they are forgiven them; if you retain the sins of any, they are retained.'

## Initial observations

The resurrection appearance narratives are unique to each gospel. This means that we are dealing with deep reflection, presented in the form of narrative, rather than with the more historical reports that we find in the Synoptic Gospels. These narratives manage to express faith in Christ risen from the dead, as well as to address issues current at the time of writing.

## Kind of writing

In John 20 – perhaps originally the final chapter – there are four resurrection appearance scenes: (1) Mary Magdalene (in two moments); (2) Peter and the beloved disciple (in between the two moments with Mary); (3) the gift of the Holy Spirit and (4) doubting Thomas, prepared for by the third scene. Scenes 1, 2 and 4 deal with how one comes to Easter faith. Scene 3 deals with the gifts of the Risen Lord to his followers, that is, the Holy Spirit and forgiveness.

## Old Testament background

(i) The first day of the week suggests creation, which began on the first day.

> In the beginning when God created the heavens and the earth, the earth was a formless void and darkness covered the face of the deep, while a wind from God swept over the face of the waters. Then God said, 'Let there be light'; and there was light. And God saw

that the light was good; and God separated the light from the darkness. God called the light Day, and the darkness he called Night. And there was evening and there was morning, the first day. (Genesis 1:1–5)

(ii) Peace (*shalom*) has a special range of meanings in the Old Testament: fertility, health, prosperity, good relationships (see Psalm 122). Victory over death is included here.

> Pray for the peace of Jerusalem: 'May they prosper who love you. Peace be within your walls, and security within your towers.' For the sake of my relatives and friends I will say, 'Peace be within you.' For the sake of the house of the LORD our God, I will seek your good. (Psalm 122:6–9)

## New Testament foreground

i)  This gospel uses the *topos* of the new creation to frame the story of Jesus. It starts with 'in the beginning'. On the cross Jesus' words echo 'when God had finished' on the sixth day. The Easter stories are twice signalled to be 'on the first day of the week' and in today's story, Jesus, echoing the Creator in Genesis 2, breathes on the disciples.

(ii) The phrase 'just as' echoes important themes in the Fourth Gospel. In general the point being made is that Jesus does not simply set an example that they should follow, but that Jesus' example enables the following. This means that believers do not simply 'copy', but are enabled to do as Jesus did by the gift of the Risen Lord and the power of the Holy Spirit. See these texts:

> For I have set you an example, that you also should do *just as* I have done to you. (John 13:15, adjusted)

> Little children, I am with you only a little longer. You will look for me; and as I said to the Jews so now

I say to you, 'Where I am going, you cannot come. I give you a new commandment, that you love one another. *Just as* I have loved you, you also should love one another.' (John 13:33–34)

Abide in me as I abide in you. *Just as* the branch cannot bear fruit by itself unless it abides in the vine, neither can you unless you abide in me. (John 15:4)

*Just as* the Father has loved me, so I have loved you; abide in my love. If you keep my commandments, you will abide in my love, *just as* I have kept my Father's commandments and abide in his love. I have said these things to you so that my joy may be in you, and that your joy may be complete. (John 15:9–11 adjusted)

'This is my commandment, that you love one another *just as* I have loved you. (John 15:12 adjusted)

And now I am no longer in the world, but they are in the world, and I am coming to you. Holy Father, protect them in your name that you have given me, so that they may be one, as we are one. *Just as* you have sent me into the world, so I have sent them into the world. (John 17:11, 18 adjusted)

*Just as* you, Father, are in me and I am in you, may they also be in us, so that the world may believe that you have sent me. The glory that you have given me I have given them, so that they may be one, as we are one, I in them and you in me, that they may become completely one, so that the world may know that you have sent me and have loved them *just as* you have loved me. (John 17:21–23 adjusted)

## St Paul

> So then, brothers and sisters, we are debtors, not to the flesh, flesh, you will die; but if by the Spirit you put to death the deeds of the body, you will live. For all who are led by the Spirit of God are children of God. For you did not receive a spirit of slavery to fall back into fear, but you have received a spirit of adoption. When we cry, 'Abba! Father!' it is that very Spirit bearing witness with our spirit that we are children of God, and if children, then heirs, heirs of God and joint heirs with Christ – if, in fact, we suffer with him so that we may also be glorified with him. (Romans 8:12–17)

## Brief commentary

### (V. 19)

It does not say immediately 'the twelve,' which would emphasise authority, but rather 'the disciples', which underscores attachment to Jesus. As often in John, we are meant to think of the historical disciples of Jesus of Nazareth as well as the present readers, who are disciples of the Risen Lord. Jesus 'comes' in John – something special to him. This recalls: *I will not leave you orphaned; I am coming to you* (John 14:18). *Peace I leave with you; my peace I give to you. I do not give to you as the world gives. Do not let your hearts be troubled, and do not let them be afraid. You heard me say to you, 'I am going away, and I am coming to you.' If you loved me, you would rejoice that I am going to the Father, because the Father is greater than I* (John 14:27–28).

### (V. 20)

In Luke, Jesus shows his hands and his feet, to show that it really is himself indeed. This motif is developed in John, who reminds us not only of the manner of death, but the spring of salvation, the water of life which flowed from the side of Jesus. Thus, both the death of Jesus and its efficacy are presented. Again unlike in Luke, there is no hesitation, but rather complete joy as they 'see' the Lord in that full sense the word has in John's Gospel. This deep seeing fulfils the words of Jesus, *In a little while the world will no longer see me, but you will see me; because I live, you also will live. On that day you will know that I am in my Father, and you in me, and I in you* (John 14:19–20). Even the perfection of joy has been anticipated by Jesus in the Gospel: *So you have pain now; but I will see you again, and your hearts will rejoice, and no one will take your joy from you. Until now you have not asked for anything in my name. Ask and you will receive, so that your joy may be complete* (John 16:22, 24).

(V. 21)

Just as in the Old Testament, a theophany always means a task or a call, likewise in the New Testament, the Risen Lord has roles for his followers. Theirs will be the task to bring to the world the riches and blessings achieved by the Risen Lord. The first sentence sends them out and the second sentence makes the mission possible. The note 'just as' is stronger than a comparison – it means there is a direct continuity between the first and second sendings. The gesture of breathing is taken from Genesis 2:7.

(V. 22)

This verb 'to breathe' is used only here in the New Testament and is a direct echo of the Old Testament usage, as just noted. The rereading in Wisdom 15:10–11 is close to John because it links the verb to inspire, to breathe into, which is based on the root *pneuma*, meaning breath or wind. At this moment, the new creation comes to be. It is likewise a fulfilment of a prediction of John the Baptist: *And John testified, 'I saw the Spirit descending from heaven like a dove, and it remained on him. I myself did not know him, but the one who sent me to baptise with water said to me, 'He on whom you see the Spirit descend and remain is the one who baptises with the Holy Spirit'* (John 1:32–33).

(V. 23)

Of course, this gift of the Spirit is given to all and has nothing to do with a special gift to the apostles and even less to do with ordination. The Spirit is given to all, as we read: *By this we know that we abide in him and he in us, because he has given us of his Spirit* (1 John 4:13). This joining of the Risen Christ and the gift of the Spirit prevents any separation of the age of the Son from the age of the Spirit. The unexpected word about forgiveness of sins (in the plural) echoes something in Matthew 18:18 *Truly I tell you, whatever you bind on earth will be bound in heaven, and whatever you loose on earth will be loosed in heaven.* Within a resurrection appearance story, the mission to preach forgiveness of sins is found elsewhere – cf. Luke 24:27; Matthew 28:19 and even Mark 16:16, if you must. But this is the only mention of forgiveness in the Fourth Gospel. As there is no 'clergy' in the Johannine community, the gift of forgiveness is given to the community or the church (or assembly) as a whole.

## Pointers for prayer

a) Jesus comes into a room full of fear. Sometimes it is fear itself that makes us close the door on others and on God. Occasionally a person comes along with the gift of breaking through our closed doors, a person who comes to be with us in our fears. Do you have memories of people getting through to you and being with you despite your closed doors? Who brought you peace in a time of anxiety?

b) Jesus showed his wounds to his friends. Moments of grace can occur when others show us their vulnerable side, or when we do that with them. Let your memories speak of such experiences to you.

c) As Jesus was sent by the Father, so he sent out the disciples. This evokes images of receiving and handing on the things that give life: values, meaning, sense of purpose, love. Who are the people who gave you life by what they handed on to you? To whom have you handed on what is life-giving?

d) In our tradition the final verse reminds us of the Sacrament of Reconciliation but its meaning is broader than that. Spirit-filled people are people who forgive. You might like to recall memories of when you have forgiven, or retained, another's sins. What difference has it made to you and others when you forgive rather than hold sins against others?

## Prayer

*Send down, O God, upon your people the flame of your Holy Spirit, and fill with the abundance of your sevenfold gift the Church you brought forth from your Son's pierced side.*

*May your life-giving Spirit lend fire to our words and strength to our witness.*

*Send us forth to the nations of the world to proclaim with boldness your wondrous work of raising Christ to your right hand.*

*We make our prayer through our Lord Jesus Christ, your Son, who lives and reigns with you in the unity of the Holy Spirit, God for ever and ever. Amen.*

## 🌿 Second Reading 🌿

**1 Cor 12:1** *Now concerning spiritual gifts, brothers and sisters, I do not want you to be uninformed.* [2] *You know that when you were pagans, you were enticed and led astray to idols that could not speak.* [3] Therefore I want you to understand that no one speaking by the Spirit of God ever says 'Let Jesus be cursed!' and no one can say 'Jesus is Lord' except by the Holy Spirit.

[4] Now there are varieties of gifts, but the same Spirit; [5] and there are varieties of services, but the same Lord; [6] and there are varieties of activities, but it is the same God who activates all of them in everyone. [7] To each is given the manifestation of the Spirit for the common good.

[12] For just as the body is one and has many members, and all the members of the body, though many, are one body, so it is

with Christ. [13] For in the one Spirit we were all baptised into one body – Jews or Greeks, slaves or free – and we were all made to drink of one Spirit.

## Initial observations

This is a wonderful passage for the feast of Pentecost, taking us to the very heart of what it means to be community. The ideal can still inspire and keep us focused on what truly matters.

## Kind of writing

In this great letter, chs 12, 13 and 14 belong properly together, dealing in turn with diversity, love and order. Diversity is evident (12); less evident is the one giver of all the gifts. The actual order of things (14) constitutes a practical application of the principle of love so marvellously developed in chapter 13. The grand structure is both evident and important: ABA'.

The careful presentation of Paul's teaching in ch. 12 shows the following steps:

1–3:     *Introduction*
4–11:    charisms, prophecy and tongues
12–26:   the metaphor of the body
27–31:   charisms, prophecy and tongues.

As is immediately evident, after the introductory verses, this chapter itself falls into a concentric pattern (ABA'). The edited excerpt takes v. 3 from the introduction and vv. 12–13 from the middle section. The opening two verses are included here for the sake of completeness.

## Origin of the reading

The context in the community is conflict – to us a peculiar kind of competition over the spiritual gifts. Being superior in prayer can be a seductive sin under the guise of grace.

Even though the issue is quite local to the Corinthian community, the experience of diversity *and conflict* is normal to all assemblies and the principles behind our real communion are surely valid and practical up to today.

## Related passages

> For by the grace given to me I say to everyone among you not to think of yourself more highly than you ought to think, but to think with sober judgment, each according to the measure of faith that God has assigned. For as in one body we have many members, and not all the members have the same function, so we, who are many, are one body in Christ, and individually we are members one of another. We have gifts that differ according to the grace given to us: prophecy, in proportion to faith; ministry, in ministering; the teacher, in teaching; the exhorter, in exhortation; the giver, in generosity; the leader, in diligence; the compassionate, in cheerfulness. (Romans 12:3–8)

> By contrast, the fruit of the Spirit is love, joy, peace, patience, kindness, generosity, faithfulness, gentleness and self-control. There is no law against such things. And those who belong to Christ Jesus have crucified the flesh with its passions and desires. If we live by the Spirit, let us also be guided by the Spirit. Let us not become conceited, competing against one another, envying one another. (Galatians 5:22–26)

## Brief commentary

(V. 1)
A new section is marked by two indicators: firstly, 'now concerning', and, secondly, the double negative of *not* wanting them to be *uninformed*.

(V. 2)
Paul reminds them where they have come from by underlining the inability of their previous 'gods' to speak at all, in contrast to the plethora

of 'speaking gifts'. It is a subtle hint that when they, the Corinthians, speak in tongues or in prophecy, it is really God who is speaking. Taking credit for it or even being proud of it, therefore, has no place whatsoever.

(V. 3)

Paul gives an example, which is in part problematic. Paul's main point here is that the general confession of faith is inspired by the Spirit, common to all Christians without distinction and focused on Jesus, crucified and risen. As for 'cursed (literally anathema) [be] Jesus', it might be (a) a misunderstanding of Paul's teaching (see Galatians 3:13, but the word cursed is different), or (b) a deliberately disturbing sentence to show that not everything uttered ecstatically may be attributed to the Spirit.

(Vv. 4–6)

These two lines are quite poetic even in English. Each affirmation starts, in Greek, with the word *diairesis*, which means both distribution and difference. The NJB gets nearest to conveying both meanings: *There are many different gifts, but it is always the same Spirit* (1 Corinthians 12:4). The emphasis on the *giver* prohibits any claim that this is our own. Furthermore, the emphasis on the *same* giver throughout leads to the key affirmation in v. 7. As for activating all of them in everyone: see 1 Corinthians 8:6; Romans 11:36 and even Acts 17:25.

(V. 7)

'My' gift is never really for me alone. Cf. *So with yourselves; since you are eager for spiritual gifts, strive to excel in them for building up the church* (1 Corinthians 14:12).

(V. 12)

The metaphor is not original to Paul but comes from the politics and (Stoic) philosophy of the time. In that context, the usual use was to know your place and, even more important, to stay in it! Paul is radically different: all members are equal and in any case it is the body *of Christ*.

(V. 13)

Again, in his affirmations, Paul underlines what is common to all, in contrast to elitist pretensions. The radical Paul is evident: all have the

Spirit equally, fully and without distinction, whatever about the particular *manifestation* of the Spirit given to some. It would be consistent for Paul to be thinking of both baptism and Eucharist (drink) at this point. Cf. *For all who eat and drink without discerning the body, eat and drink judgment against themselves* (1 Corinthians 11:29).

## Pointers for prayer

a) When free from possessiveness and pretension, the recognition of the gifts can be a source of life and joy.

b) Can I name my own sense of belonging as a Christian? What are my gifts? With whom do I share them?

## Prayer

*Loving God, in the Spirit you call us into fellowship and communion. We thank you for your different gifts to each and all. As we recognise you, the one giver, may we imitate you in the building up of all without difference or distinction. Through Christ our Lord. Amen.*

## 🍃 First Reading 🍃

**Acts 2:1** When the day of Pentecost had come, they were all together in one place. ² And suddenly from heaven there came a sound like the rush of a violent wind, and it filled the entire house where they were sitting. ³ Divided tongues, as of fire, appeared among them, and a tongue rested on each of them. ⁴ All of them were filled with the Holy Spirit and began to speak in other languages, as the Spirit gave them ability.

⁵ Now there were devout Jews from every nation under heaven living in Jerusalem. ⁶ And at this sound the crowd gathered and was bewildered, because each one heard them speaking in the native language of each. ⁷ Amazed and astonished, they

asked, 'Are not all these who are speaking Galileans? [8] And how is it that we hear, each of us, in our own native language? [9] Parthians, Medes, Elamites, and residents of Mesopotamia, Judea and Cappadocia, Pontus and Asia, [10] Phrygia and Pamphylia, Egypt and the parts of Libya belonging to Cyrene, and visitors from Rome, both Jews and proselytes, [11] Cretans and Arabs – in our own languages we hear them speaking about God's deeds of power.'

## Initial observations

This dramatic scene and commentary correspond in some measure to the opening tableau in Luke 4:16–30. Like that opening scene in the Gospel, the portrayal of the day of Pentecost is both synthetic and pro-grammatic. It is synthetic in that it gathers into one foundational scene the many experiences of the Holy Spirit that marked the life of the early Church. It is programmatic in that this is the scene which holds the energy behind the breathtaking expansion of the Way recounted in the Acts. Luke lays out the material is the symbolic language of forty days appearances and the outpouring of the Spirit fifty days after Passover (see below). That this is symbolic may be appreciated by noting that in John's Gospel the Spirit is given fully on Easter Sunday itself.

## Kind of writing

This is a symbolic tableau, capturing multiple experiences of the Spirit, in dialogue with Genesis 11:1–9 and Joel. It combines the two themes of the Jewish feast of Shavuot/Pentecost. (i) Harvest: Pentecost initi-ates the gathering in of the Gentiles. Harvest language always suggests sifting, i.e. judgment. (ii) The giving of the Law on Sinai: Pentecost cel-ebrated the writing of the Law on the hearts of believers (cf. Jeremiah).

## Origin of the reading

(i)  Shavuot or Pentecost was one of the three pilgrimage feast of Judaism. Legislation can be found in Exodus 23:16;

34:12; Leviticus 23:15–21; Deuteronomy 16:9–12. It was an important harvest feast, as we see from Paul's eagerness to be in Jerusalem for it (Acts 20:16). By the time of Jesus' ministry, it had also come to mark the giving of the Law, the Torah, on Mount Sinai. All the metaphors used – sound, wind and fire – have a considerable Old Testament background.

(ii) The feast is also mentioned in the *Mishnah*, in the significant context of the last judgment:

> At four seasons of the year the world is judged: at Passover for grain; at Pentecost for fruit of the tree; at the New Year all who enter the world pass before Him like troops since it is said, He who fashions the hearts of them all and who considers all their works (Psalm 33:15); and on the Festival [of Tabernacles] they are judged in regard to water. (Rosh Hashanah 1:2)

(iii) Pentecost, in Acts 2, is in dialogue with Genesis 11, the story of the Tower of Babel.

(iv) The speech that follows cites the prophet Joel 2:28–32, in the Septuagint (Greek) version, making significant adjustments.

### Related passages

There is a direct link to Luke 4:16–30. Also the story of the birth of the church in Acts is an evolution and practical development from this brief scene here. There are further 'Pentecosts' in the Acts:

> Now when the apostles at Jerusalem heard that Samaria had accepted the word of God, they sent Peter and John to them. The two went down and prayed for them that they might receive the Holy Spirit (for as yet the Spirit had not come upon any of them; they had only been baptised in the name

of the Lord Jesus). Then Peter and John laid their hands on them, and they received the Holy Spirit. (Acts 8:14–17)

While Peter was still speaking, the Holy Spirit fell upon all who heard the word. The circumcised believers who had come with Peter were astounded that the gift of the Holy Spirit had been poured out even on the Gentiles, for they heard them speaking in tongues and extolling God. (Acts 10:44–46)

While Apollos was in Corinth, Paul passed through the interior regions and came to Ephesus, where he found some disciples. He said to them, 'Did you receive the Holy Spirit when you became believers?' They replied, 'No, we have not even heard that there is a Holy Spirit.' Then he said, 'Into what then were you baptised?' They answered, 'Into John's baptism.' Paul said, 'John baptised with the baptism of repentance, telling the people to believe in the one who was to come after him, that is, in Jesus.' On hearing this, they were baptised in the name of the Lord Jesus. When Paul had laid his hands on them, the Holy Spirit came upon them, and they spoke in tongues and prophesied – altogether there were about twelve of them. (Acts 19:1–7)

## Brief commentary

(V. 1)
That is, the beginning of the Christian harvest which is the theme of Acts, taking us from Jerusalem to Rome. The languages are perhaps not meant literally. It means more that the Gospel message 'speaks' to every human heart.

(V. 2)
God as a wind/breath is found elsewhere, both in the Old Testament and the New Testament. It is invisible, unpredictable, uncontrollable and powerful. Thus it suggests itself as an image for God. This is true, yet it is not the wind that fills the house, but the sound! We are to think of an overwhelming, deafening sound.

(V. 3)

Distributed might be better than divided, because the author stresses unity throughout. Fire was equally mysterious to early humans – being apparently not a thing, yet capable of giving light and heat (positive), death and destruction (negative).

(V. 4)

Speaking in tongues was apparently a frequent phenomenon in the early church (1 Corinthians 14:1–33). 'Filled' is a fulfilment of a prediction and command of Jesus (Luke 24:49; Acts 1:4–5, 8).

(V. 5)

This suggests that we are to think not of all nations, but of Jews in these lands or among these nations. Again, he is not thinking of transient residents, but rather permanent foreign residents. The city did have a mixed population.

(V. 6)

This represents the reversal of Babel, an important clue for interpreting the Pentecost event in a universalist key.

(V. 7)

Luke uses the crowd to express appropriate reaction.

(Vv. 8–11)

The list is symbolic – because the details are problematic. For example, why Judea? Parthians and Medes were no long politically significant.

## Pointers for prayer

a) It might help to reflect on times in your own life when you experienced a special awakening and enthusiasm for the Gospel. What was going on in your life before this and what were the effects afterwards?

b) The passage from Acts includes another interpretation: they are full of new wine. Did you ever get that kind of reaction, where someone 'explained' your engagement in the faith by means of another interpretation?

c)  The gifts of the Spirit are many (see Galatians 5:22 and 1 Corinthians 12). Can I name my own gifts and give thanks to God the Holy Spirit?

## Prayer

*God of new life and new beginnings, send your Holy Spirit again upon your people gathered in prayer. Breathe into us the very breath of God, in whom we live and move and have our being.*
*Through Christ our Lord. Amen.*

## Themes across the readings

The gospel represents, in some measure, the Johannine Pentecost, on the first Easter Day. The symbolism in the Acts of the forty days to the Ascension and fifty days to Pentecost is a Lucan construction. Luke's symbolic tableau gathers together many experiences of the outpouring of the Spirit, as we saw above. Psalm 104 (103) with its universal vision makes a great response to the story of Pentecost: *Send forth your spirit, O Lord, and renew the face of the earth.*

# Chapter 10

## Holy Trinity C

### Thought for the day

'Silence is the language God speaks and everything else is a bad translation' is variously attributed. Whoever penned it, it strikes a chord on the feast of the Holy and Undivided Trinity. As we stand before the absolute mystery of God, one and three, transcendent and immanent, greater than our hearts and yet closer to us than we are to ourselves, wordless prayer is fitting. And yet ... the Mysterious Silence has been broken, if not by 'mere' words then certainly by the Word made flesh, whose Spirit has been poured into our hearts.

### Prayer

*God, beyond our minds and ideas, our hearts and our feelings, we believe absolutely in your love for each and for all. Let your astonishing love kindle in our inner selves a response of love and wonder.*
*Through Christ our Lord. Amen.*

### 🍃 Gospel 🍃

**Jn 16:12** [Jesus said:] 'I still have many things to say to you, but you cannot bear them now. [13] When the Spirit of truth comes, he will guide you into all the truth; for he will not speak on his own, but will speak whatever he hears, and he will declare to you the things that are to come. [14] He will glorify me, because he will take what is mine and declare it to you. [15] All that the Father has is mine. For this reason I said that he will take what is mine and declare it to you.'

## Initial observations

The Fourth Gospel is in two parts: The Book of Signs (1–12) and the Book of Glory (13–20+21). Within the Book of Glory, the farewell discourse of Jesus takes up most of five chapters. The outline is as follows:

THE BOOK OF GLORY (13:1–20:31)

A. The Last Discourse (13:1–17:26)

a.     Making God known: the foot washing and the morsel (13:1–38)

  b.  Departure (14:1–31)

    c.  To abide, to love, and to be hated (15:1–16:3)

  b*. Departure (16:4–33)

a*.   Making God known: Jesus' final prayer (17:1–26)

When a text is laid out in a pattern like this (a-b-c-b$^1$-a$^1$), the important question to ask is whether the physical centre of the pattern (here c. 15:1–16:3) is the centre of meaning or the heart of the matter. When the outer parts correspond (for example b and b$^1$), then the reader is entitled to read one in the light of the other.

In our case, the promise of continued presence through the Spirit is treated twice, that is, in chs 14 and 16, and these chapters ought to be read in light of each other.

## Kind of writing

The farewell speech is fairly well established as a literary genre in the Old Testament and the apocryphal books of the intertestamental period. Further details can be found in Chapter 5 of this volume.

## Old Testament background

There is an interesting and wide background to the Spirit in the Old Testament (both in Hebrew and in Greek). *The Spirit and creation*:

Genesis 1:2; Job 33:4; Psalm 104:30. The Spirit is a saving power: Exodus 14:21; 1 Kings 18:45. *The Spirit guides history and people*: Judges 3:10; 6:34; 1 Samuel 10:1–13; 16:13. The prophets are inspired by the Spirit: Isaiah 34:16; 63:10; Ezekiel 18:31. It was expected that the final, *messianic age would be the age of the Spirit*: on rulers (Isaiah 11:1–10; 42:1; 61:1); *on the whole people* (Isaiah 32:15; 44:3; Ezekiel 39:29; Joel 2:28 [3:28]); changing hearts of stone to hearts of flesh (Isaiah 59:21; Ezekiel 36:26–27). Late pre-New Testament Judaism emphasises the Spirit of prophecy, of revelation and guidance (Sirach 48:24), of wisdom (Wisdom 7:7; 9:17; 1QH 12:11–13), and occasionally of praise.

## New Testament foreground

The Holy Spirit is central to the religious imagination of the Fourth Gospel, being the link between God, the believer and Jesus. Here are some of the important texts.

> *Jesus has the Holy Spirit*: And John testified, 'I saw the Spirit descending from heaven like a dove, and it remained on him. I myself did not know him, but the one who sent me to baptise with water said to me, 'He on whom you see the Spirit descend and remain is the one who baptises with the Holy Spirit' (John 1:32–33). On the last day of the festival, the great day, while Jesus was standing there, he cried out, 'Let anyone who is thirsty come to me, and let the one who believes in me drink. As the scripture scripture has said "Out of the believer's heart shall flow rivers of living water"'. Now he said this about the Spirit, which believers in him were to receive; for as yet there was no Spirit, because Jesus was not yet glorified (John 7:37–39).

> *Jesus' death 'releases' the Holy Spirit*: When Jesus had received the wine, he said, 'It is finished.' Then he bowed his head and gave up his spirit (lit. he handed over his Spirit; John 19:30).

> *The spirit is the special gift of the Risen Lord*: Nevertheless I tell you the truth: it is to your advantage that I go away, for

if I do not go away, the Advocate will not come to you; but if I go, I will send him to you. (John 16:7) When he had said this, he breathed on them and said to them, 'Receive the Holy Spirit. If you forgive the sins of any, they are forgiven them; if you retain the sins of any, they are retained' (John 20:22–23).

*Believers are reborn in the Spirit*: Jesus answered, 'Very truly, I tell you, no one can enter the kingdom of God without being born of water and Spirit. What is born of the flesh is flesh, and what is born of the Spirit is spirit. Do not be astonished that I said to you, "You must be born from above." The wind blows where it chooses, and you hear the sound of it, but you do not know where it comes from or where it goes. So it is with everyone who is born of the Spirit' (John 3:5–8). 'But the hour is coming, and is now here, when the true worshippers will worship the Father in spirit and truth, for the Father seeks such as these to worship him. God is spirit, and those who worship him must worship in spirit and truth' (John 4:23–24).

*The Spirit/Advocate has three tasks*: And I will ask the Father, and he will give you another Advocate, to be with you forever (John 14:16). But the Advocate, the Holy Spirit, whom the Father will send in my name, will teach you everything, and remind you of all that I have said to you (John 14:26). When the Advocate comes, whom I will send to you from the Father, the Spirit of truth who comes from the Father, he will testify on my behalf (John 15:26).

## St Paul

But you are not in the flesh; you are in the Spirit, since the Spirit of God dwells in you. Anyone who does not have the Spirit of Christ does not belong to him. But if Christ is in you, though the body is dead because of sin, the Spirit is life because of righteousness. If the Spirit of him who raised Jesus from the dead dwells in you, he who raised Christ from the dead will give life to your mortal bodies also through his Spirit that dwells in you. (Romans 8:9–11)

Likewise the Spirit helps us in our weakness; for we do not know how to pray as we ought, but that very Spirit intercedes with sighs too deep for words. And God, who searches the heart, knows what is the mind of the Spirit, because the Spirit intercedes for the saints according to the will of God. (Romans 8:26–27)

## Brief commentary

(V. 12)
Understanding later is a key feature of this gospel: John 2:22; 12:16; 14:25–26, 16:12–13; 20:9. This developed emphasis surely reflects the experience of the first generation of believers as they read the ministry in the light of the resurrection. 'Now' continues the fiction that these words – from the hand of the evangelist – go back to the actual time before the death of Jesus.

(V. 13)
Spirit and truth are closely connected in the Johannine writings: John 4:23–24; 14:17; 15:26; 16:13; 1 John 4:6; 5:6. 'Truth' here is interpersonal and even personal, because Jesus himself, in this gospel, is the way, the truth and the life: Jesus said to him, 'I am the way, and the truth, and the life. No one comes to the Father except through me' (John 14:6).

(V. 14)
In this gospel glory and glorification do not refer to honour or reputation etc. Instead, glory is a category that has to do with revelation, precisely the revelation of God's compassionate love through the lifting up of Jesus on the cross and into the resurrection. 'He will glorify me' needs to be translated as follows: The function of the Holy Spirit is to bring into the hearts of believers that very love between Jesus and the Father, so

that God's compassionate love, revealed through the Paschal Mystery, may live in the centre of our being. In that exhilarating sense, 'he will take what is mine and declare it to you'.

(V. 15)
This wonderful gift of relationship takes us back to the Father: 'For God so loved the world that he gave his only Son, so that everyone who believes in him may not perish but may have eternal life' (John 3:16).

## Pointers for prayer

a) Wisdom about life comes slowly and sometimes painfully. Hearing the 'right' answer at the 'wrong' time does not help us. We need to be ready and open to receiving the truth if it is to have any impact. Perhaps you can recall some occasions when it was the 'right' time for you to learn a truth about life. Remember your experiences of growing in understanding and truth.

b) Perhaps the Spirit guided you through the words of someone close to you, or through the words and actions of people you read about or saw on TV. Or maybe understanding came to you when praying or reflecting on your life. Remember and give thanks for the people who have helped you to greater wisdom on your journey through life.

c) Wisdom is handed on from person to person, and from generation to generation, within families, within communities etc. Are there any particular gems of wisdom that you cherish from what has been handed on to you?

## Prayer

*God, your name is veiled in mystery, yet we dare to call you Father; your Son was begotten before all ages, yet is born among us in time; your Holy Spirit fills the whole creation, yet is poured forth now into our hearts.*

*Because you have made us and loved us and called us by your name, draw us more deeply into your divine life, that we may glorify you rightly, through your Son, in the unity of the Holy Spirit, God, for ever and ever. Amen.*

## 🌿 Second Reading 🌿

**Romans 5:1** Therefore, since we are justified by *faith*, we have peace with God through our Lord Jesus Christ, ² through whom we have obtained access to this grace in which we stand; and we boast in our *hope* of sharing the glory of God. ³ And not only that, but we also boast in our sufferings, knowing that suffering produces endurance, ⁴ and endurance produces character, and character produces hope, ⁵ and hope does not disappoint us, because God's *love* has been poured into our hearts through the Holy Spirit that has been given to us.

## Initial observations

Our reading for the feast is especially well chosen. It brings together in a kind of experiential way the persons of the Trinity. Paul, of course, would never have used such a term, but in texts like these you can see the seeds of the later doctrine.

## Kind of writing

In the broadest terms, the letter to the Romans unfolds in four major moments:

1–4: all have sinned; all in need of grace
5–8: God's grace in Christ
9–11: Jews and Gentiles in God's plan
12–15: How to live tolerantly

Our reading comes from step 2. At this point, Paul parades all that Christians have received in Christ – salvation, faith, baptism, the continued moral struggle, Abba Father, the Holy Spirit and unshakeable faith in Christ. It is a mighty display, in the light of which the various divisions and differences are reduced to insignificance. It is a kind of implied *a fortiori* argument: with so much in common ... and useful today!

The key Pauline triad of faith, hope and love is present here, in the same order as in 1 Corinthians 13:13 (contrast 1 Thessalonians 1:3; 5:8). We may note, finally, that this whole argument from 5 to 8 is framed by affirmations about the God, Christ and the Spirit.

## Origin of the reading

Paul wrote to the Romans to help them resolve an issue that was central to his own mission: how both Jews and Gentiles might live in communion and in mutual respect. The specific challenge goes back to how much of Jewish traditional practice may be retained and, perhaps, imposed. In the mind of Paul, the so-called identity markers of Judaism – setting apart God's chosen people – simply no longer make sense in the light of Jesus' death and resurrection. Now that God has extended his covenant and opened his grace to all 'without distinction', such separation is not only not necessary but it even betrays a failure to understand God's project in Jesus.

## Related passages

> No, in all these things we are more than conquerors through him who loved us. For I am convinced that neither death, nor life, nor angels, nor rulers, nor things present, nor things to come, nor powers, nor height, nor depth, nor anything else in all creation, will be able to separate us from the love of God in Christ Jesus our Lord. (Romans 8:37–39)

> Not that I have already obtained this or have already reached the goal; but I press on to make it my own, because Christ Jesus has made me his own. Beloved, I do not consider that I have made it my own; but this one thing I do: forgetting what lies behind and straining forward to what lies ahead, I press on towards the goal for the prize of the heavenly call of God in Christ Jesus. (Philippians 3:12–14)

## Brief commentary

(V. 1)

The second major section of the letter starts here with 'therefore'. The very first word in Greek is 'justified', emphatically located.

'By faith' has two meanings. By the faith and fidelity of Jesus, God brought about our salvation. By our faith, that is by our trust in God who raised Jesus, we enter into that salvation. Peace is a summary word, with all its range of meanings in the Hebrew Bible, and, at the same time, an objective word describing the new situation of humanity in Christ. Notice the 'we have'. Many manuscripts and some translations have 'let us have'. The indicative is likely to be correct.

(V. 2)

Access is a fairly rare word which can also be translated as approach. Grace is a huge topic in Paul. The base meaning is favour or gift. It is used in the Old Testament to speak of God's election, based precisely on his gracious love. In the New Testament, it can mean God's initiative, God's call and God's gifts in the charismata. Here, the chief sense is God's gracious achievement in Christ. The corresponding human response is faith.

The temporal markers are important here. Paul does believe in the events of salvation as an objective reality already achieved in Christ. In the present, believers really live this reality, but not yet fully. The old 'already-and-not-yet' should be kept in mind. Paul has a very strong tension towards the future completion of salvation. He is also sharply aware that becoming a disciple is never over, as we see in the next few verses (cf. Philippians 3:12–14).

Elsewhere, Paul prohibits boasting, as a human achievement, but, of course, we may properly be confident and even boast of God's action in Christ.

(Vv. 3–5a)

Even though so much has been bestowed upon us, we suffer and we struggle. Paul's literary skill is evident here as he combines concatenated conjunctions with supple use of anadiplosis (= last word of a phrase taken up at the start of the next). Paul makes it clear that salvation is still a process, open to conversion and open to the future.

(V. 5b)

'Love of God' has two meanings, both of which are present here. The primary meaning is God's love for us on the basis of which we are enabled to love God. Cf. 1 John 4:19 for the same teaching. For the pouring out of the Spirit see for example Isaiah 32:15 and Joel 2:28–29. For love at the end of Romans 8, see the citation above.

## Pointers for prayer

a) Paul's awareness of the grace/gift helps us to recognise, joyfully, all we have received.

b) Has it been my experience that suffering and endurance can be positive?

## Prayer

*God of every grace and gift, we come before you in gratitude and great joy. Send your Holy Spirit once more into our hearts and lives that we may truly know your love and come to love you by the power of the same Holy Spirit. Through Christ our Lord. Amen.*

## 🌿 First Reading 🌿

**Proverbs 8:22** The LORD created me at the beginning of his work,

the first of his acts of long ago.

23    Ages ago I was set up,

at the first, before the beginning of the earth.

24    When there were no depths I was brought forth,

when there were no springs abounding with water.

25    Before the mountains had been shaped,

before the hills, I was brought forth –

26    when he had not yet made earth and fields,
        or the world's first bits of soil.
27    When he established the heavens, I was there,
        when he drew a circle on the face of the deep,
28    when he made firm the skies above,
        when he established the fountains of the deep,
29    when he assigned to the sea its limit,
        so that the waters might not transgress his command,
    when he marked out the foundations of the earth,
30      then I was beside him, like a master worker;
    and I was daily his delight,
        rejoicing before him always,
31    rejoicing in his inhabited world
        and delighting in the human race.

## Initial observations

It has long been recognised that Wisdom speculation and, in particular, the personification of *Lady Wisdom*, lie behind some key Christologies of the New Testament: for example, Paul, John, Colossians and Ephesians. Our reading is chosen to show this earlier expression of God's presence in all there is (panentheism, really). It is not so strange if we recall the speech of Paul on the Areopagus: *For 'In him we live and move and have our being'* (Acts 17:28).

## Kind of writing

It is poetry, showing the usual mark of parallelism. The tone of self praise may seem odd, but in fact it is common in the literature of Egypt, Mesopotamia, Greece and Rome. Technically, it is an *aretology*, or poem in the first person, in which a divine figure lists his or her attributes. The layout of ch. 8 is:

Introduction (vv. 1–3); the speech, in three main parts (vv. 4–11, 12–21, 22–31) and the conclusion of the speech (vv. 32–36).

*Layout of the book of Proverbs*

| I | 1–9 | The proverbs of Solomon son of David |
|---|-----|--------------------------------------|
| II | 10:1–22:16 | The proverbs of Solomon |
| III | 22:17–24:22 | Give ear, listen to the sayings of the sages |
| IV | 24:23–34 | The following are also taken from the sages |
| V | 25–29 | Here are some more of Solomon's proverbs |
| VI | 30:1–16 | The sayings of Agur son of Jakeh, of Massa |
| VII | 30:17–33 | Numerical Proverbs |
| VIII | 31:1–9 | The sayings of Lemuel, king of Massa |
| IX | 31:10–31 | The Perfect Housewife |

## Origin of the reading

Our passage crowns the opening section of the book from chs 1 to 9. Proverbs does contain real proverbs, but our passage is really 'court wisdom', the product of education and study. The teaching of an organising principle through creation is not at all unique to the Hebrew Scriptures but is part of wider ancient Near East speculation.

## Related passages

There is a highly significant Old Testament background to the figure of Lady Wisdom. She represents an attempt to speak of God as both present (immanent) and beyond (transcendent) and yet present in all that is (panentheistic).

Every faith has to 'negotiate' this and Christians did it later with the doctrines of the incarnation and the Trinity. Some examples here may help: one is from the Hebrew Bible (MT) and the other is from the Greek Old Testament, the Septuagint (LXX). These are important passages for the seeds of later doctrines.

Wisdom is portrayed as a woman, because just as men and women complete each other, wisdom completes the human being. In the culture, women were associated with fundamental needs: shelter, nourishment and companionship (and Wisdom, metaphorically). See especially Proverbs 8 and Sirach 24.

Does not wisdom call, and does not understanding raise her voice? On the heights, beside the way, at the crossroads she takes her stand; beside the gates in front of the town, at the entrance of the portals she cries out: 'To you, O people, I call, and my cry is to all that live.' (Proverbs 8:1–4)

Wisdom praises herself, and tells of her glory in the midst of her people. In the assembly of the Most High she opens her mouth, and in the presence of his hosts she tells of her glory: 'I came forth from the mouth of the Most High, and covered the earth like a mist. I dwelt in the highest heavens, and my throne was in a pillar of cloud. Alone I compassed the vault of heaven and traversed the depths of the abyss. Over waves of the sea, over all the earth, and over every people and nation I have held sway. (Sirach 24:1–6)

## Brief commentary

(Vv. 22–23)
The pre-existence of Wisdom is the foundation for her special 'know-ledge'.

(V. 24)
Again, Wisdom somehow precedes creation proper, because she is really part of God.

(Vv. 25–26)
Even in translation, there is a hint of the feminine here because the verb is used mostly of women giving birth. Back to the very basics of crea-tion, really. The ambiguity of the when of Wisdom's birth is intentional.

(V. 27)
The circle on the face of the deep indicates either the flat earth or its horizon. Wisdom was beside the Creator *before creation*, although she herself comes from God.

(V. 28)
The world picture of water below and above is the usual one, insofar

as it can be reconstructed. We should not think this too odd, given our climate, at least in Ireland!

(V. 29)
The ancient symbol of watery chaos is tamed by the mere word of the Lord, as a parent commands a child.

(V. 30)
Two images, that of a construction engineer and that of a beloved child. Somehow, God creates with the help of Wisdom, always at his side. Through her, God is present in all that is. The vision is panentheistic, as distinguished from pantheistic, that is, God cannot be reduced to all that is but, nevertheless, is present in all that is.

(V. 31)
A marvellous summary of divine delight in all that is. cf. *You spare all things, for they are yours, O Lord, you who love the living* (Wisdom 11:26).

## Pointers for prayer

a) God is all that is – recall an 'epiphany' in nature that somehow stayed with you.

b) God's delight is something we don't often think of – it includes you, believe it or not!

c) Ever since the creation of the world his eternal power and divine nature, invisible though they are, have been understood and seen through the things he has made. (Romans 1:20)

## Prayer

*God, taking delight in all you made, give us eyes to see you present in the constant wonder of creation, for in you we live and move and have our being. Through Christ our Lord. Amen.*

## Themes across the readings

The Wisdom tradition is appealing to us today – both for the spirituality and the cosmology. After the biblical period, it evolved in several directions, including towards the incarnation – the Word made flesh – and also towards the Holy Spirit and sometimes towards the Blessed Virgin Mary. Psalm 8 fits the first reading very well with its response: *How great is your name, O Lord our God, through all the earth!*

# Chapter 11

## Corpus Christi C

### Thought for the day

Bodily hunger and thirst are easy to recognise – we feel them directly. The deeper hungers can take longer, especially in our 'culture of distraction', where there is so little room for reflection and real conversation. These hungers are just as real, of course, and call for recognition and response. But the first step is really awareness and attention to the hints and nudges life provides.

### Prayer

*Help us, provider God, to recognise the hungers of the heart and not to ignore them, for in them we find our way to you, our source of life. Like plants seeking water and drawn to the light, let us be drawn to you, Creator, Father, lover. Through Christ our Lord. Amen.*

### Gospel

**Lk 9:10** *On their return the apostles told Jesus all they had done. He took them with him and withdrew privately to a city called Bethsaida.* [11] When the crowds found out about it, they followed him; and he welcomed them, and spoke to them about the kingdom of God, and healed those who needed to be cured.

[12] The day was drawing to a close, and the twelve came to him and said, 'Send the crowd away, so that they may go into

the surrounding villages and countryside, to lodge and get provisions; for we are here in a deserted place.' [13] But he said to them, 'You give them something to eat.' They said, 'We have no more than five loaves and two fish – unless we are to go and buy food for all these people.' [14] For there were about five thousand men. And he said to his disciples, 'Make them sit down in groups of about fifty each.' [15] They did so and made them all sit down. [16] And taking the five loaves and the two fish, he looked up to heaven, and blessed and broke them, and gave them to the disciples to set before the crowd. [17] And all ate and were filled. What was left over was gathered up, twelve baskets of broken pieces.

## Initial observations

The multiplication of the loaves is a natural choice for Corpus Christi. The lectionary excerpt begins at v. 11, but the story really starts at v. 10, so it is included above in italics. This story is told no fewer than six times in the New Testament, twice in both Mark and Matthew, and once each in John and Luke. The key, when reading shared accounts, is to pay attention to what is distinctive to each one. In our case, two things stand out. Firstly, Luke brings out the Eucharistic symbolism more strongly. Secondly, he underscores the intermediary role of the Twelve, as he looks ahead to their importance in the Acts. Overall, Luke is very attached to Elijah/Elisha symbolism, which comes out in this story.

## Kind of writing

The story forms an important bridge in Luke's narrative between the question raised in 9:9 ('Who is this?') and the confession in 9:20. The evocation of the Eucharist was already present in Mark's version, so that, by the time Luke's version received this tradition, it is already being read in another register. The symbolism of the account(s) makes it difficult to get back to an original tradition, not to speak of an original 'event'. Any literalist 'down-reading' – such as they shared their sandwiches – is to be strenuously resisted, of course!

## Old Testament background

There are substantial echoes in this text of the story of the manna in the desert: Exodus 16 and Numbers 11. In particular, the miracles of Elijah and Elisha should be noticed. The Gospel of Luke frequently underlines and echoes the Elijah traditions and expansions.

> Elijah said to her, 'Do not be afraid; go and do as you have said; but first make me a little cake of it and bring it to me, and afterwards make something for yourself and your son. For thus says the Lord the God of Israel: The jar of meal will not be emptied and the jug of oil will not fail until the day that the Lord sends rain on the earth.' She went and did as Elijah said, so that she as well as he and her household ate for many days. The jar of meal was not emptied, neither did the jug of oil fail, according to the word of the Lord that he spoke by Elijah. (1 Kings 17:13–16)

> A man came from Baal-shalishah, bringing food from the first fruits to the man of God: twenty loaves of barley and fresh ears of grain in his sack. Elisha said, 'Give it to the people and let them eat.' But his servant said, 'How can I set this before a hundred people?' So he repeated, 'Give it to the people and let them eat, for thus says the Lord, "They shall eat and have some left."' He set it before them, they ate, and had some left, according to the word of the Lord. (2 Kings 4:42–44)

> 'You should also look for able men among all the people, men who fear God, are trustworthy, and hate dishonest gain; set such men over them as officers over thousands, hundreds, fifties and tens. Let them sit as judges for the people at all times; let them bring every important case to you, but decide every minor case themselves. So it will be easier for you, and they will bear the burden with you. If you do this, and God so commands you, then you will be able to

endure, and all these people will go to their home in peace.'

So Moses listened to his father-in-law and did all that he had said. Moses chose able men from all Israel and appointed them as heads over the people, as officers over thousands, hundreds, fifties and tens. (Exodus 18:21–25)

## New Testament foreground

*Reversal of poverty is part of the vision of the kingdom, as we see:*

He has brought down the powerful from their thrones, and lifted up the lowly; he has filled the hungry with good things, and sent the rich away empty. (Luke 1:52–53)

'Blessed are you who are hungry now, for you will be filled. Blessed are you who weep now, for you will laugh.' (Luke 6:21)

*Meals are really significant in Luke's Gospel – Jesus is shown eating twice as frequently as in Mark and the tradition continues in the Acts of the Apostles. Two texts may illustrate:*

When he was at the table with them, he took bread, blessed and broke it, and gave it to them. Then their eyes were opened, and they recognised him; and he vanished from their sight. They said to each other, 'Were not our hearts burning within us while he was talking to us on the road, while he was opening the scriptures to us?' (Luke 24:30–32)

'We are witnesses to all that he did both in Judea and in Jerusalem. They put him to death by hanging him on a tree; but God raised him on the third day and allowed him to appear, not to all the people but to us who were chosen by God as witnesses, and who ate and drank with him after he rose from the dead.' (Acts 10:39–41)

## St Paul

> The point is this: the one who sows sparingly will also reap sparingly, and the one who sows bountifully will also reap bountifully. Each of you must give as you have made up your mind, not reluctantly or under compulsion, for God loves a cheerful giver. And God is able to provide you with every blessing in abundance, so that by always having enough of everything, you may share abundantly in every good work. As it is written, 'He scatters abroad, he gives to the poor; his righteousness endures for ever.' He who supplies seed to the sower and bread for food will supply and multiply your seed for sowing and increase the harvest of your righteousness. (2 Corinthians 9:6–10)

## Brief commentary

(V. 10)
In the different gospels the story is variously located. Only Luke has the reference to Bethsaida at the start (Mark 6:45 does refer to it, but at the end). At this point, Luke leaves out a great part of Mark – the so-called Great Omission – Mark 6:45–8:26, which began and ended with a reference to Bethsaida. Already in Mark, these stories form the background to Jesus' identity and in his own way Luke follows Mark's impulse.

(V. 11)
In Luke's telling, the crowds really are 'Gospel greedy', as we say, and they come for Jesus' message and for healing. Oddly, Luke omits Mark's mention of compassion and their being like sheep without a shepherd, a theme surely appealing to him.

(V. 12)
The time marker reminds us of Luke 24:29. The Twelve take the initiative here. Their concern expresses a compassion for the poor and the hungry (see also Acts 2:42, 4:34; 6:1–6 and 11:27–29). Their advice is

certainly practical, apart from finding the money!

**(V. 13)**

Jesus responds with a challenge. Then we learn the actual resources present – not absolutely nothing, but well short of adequate. The apostles are still thinking on a very material level. For Luke, interestingly, the Twelve themselves have this resource, unlike in the other tellings. The irony of the 200 denarii is omitted by Luke. The imperative makes a link with Elisha (see above). Why fish has puzzled commentators. There are tenuous links with Jewish tradition – not only water from the rock but fish in the water! It was certainly an early Christian symbol, but how early is difficult to establish. It may simply be that the various stories of the multiplication go back to a symbolic eschatological meal, held on the shore of the Sea of Galilee, with fish in abundance. This prophetic action of Jesus was then rewoven with themes from the Old Testament and the practice of the Lord's Supper, finally becoming the familiar 'miracle' story.

**(Vv. 14–15)**

Luke goes for the greater numbers, so as to underline the wonderful nature of the feeding of so many. The groups of fifty may echo the organisation of Israel in the desert: see Exodus 18:21–25 above. As an aside, Luke also likes 'fifty' as a number: Luke 7:41; 9:14; 16:6; Acts 13:20; 19:19. The particular verb to sit is found only in Luke in the New Testament: Luke 7:36 (Pharisee); 9:14–15 (miracle); 14:8 (parable); 24:30 (Emmaus).

**(V. 16)**

Here we have a clear and intentional echo of the Eucharistic worship of the early church. As we know, the gospels were written not only in the light of the resurrection, but also under the influence of early church traditions. Cf. 'Then he took a loaf of bread, and when he had given thanks, he broke it and gave it to them, saying, "This is my body, which is given for you. Do this in remembrance of me"' (Luke 22:19).

Luke's redaction of Mark is very clear here. Compare:

Then he ordered the crowd to sit down on the ground; and

> he took the seven loaves, and after giving thanks he broke
> them and gave them to his disciples to distribute; and they
> distributed them to the crowd. (Mark 8:6; cf. Luke 22:19)

*Looked up to heaven*: cf. Job 22:26–27, in the Greek Old Testament
(LXX). It underlines the context of prayer, which fits Luke's portrait of
Jesus as a man of prayer.

  *Gave them to the disciples to set before the crowd:* the intermediary role
of the Twelve anticipates their importance in the Acts later on.

(V. 17)

The first part of this verse describes extravagance associated with the
end of time. Cf. 'On this mountain the Lord of hosts will make for all
peoples a feast of rich food, a feast of well-aged wines, of rich food filled
with marrow, of well-aged wines strained clear' (Isaiah 25:6). Luke, in
the Greek, moves the expression 'all' to a position of emphasis – something to consider in the light of the all/many translation in the words of
institution at Mass.

  In Luke's view, the church's ministry of feeding the hungry stands
between Jesus' own ministry and its fulfilment in the heavenly banquet.
The mention of twelve baskets (rather than seven in Gentile symbolism) underscores the fulfilment of precisely Jewish expectation.

## Pointers for prayer

a) Jesus welcomes the crowd, teaches them, and cures those in
   need of healing. Bring to mind the ways in which the story
   of Jesus and his message have brought you enlightenment
   and healing.

b) The miracle is symbolic of the abundance of blessings
   coming to us from God through Jesus. How has your faith in
   Jesus been a source of nourishment to you? What blessings
   have you received through your faith?

c) When the disciples became aware of the problem they
   wanted to send the crowd away and Jesus told them 'You

give them something to eat'. They thought what they had was insufficient but Jesus used the little they had to feed the crowd. Have you ever found that when you gave the little you have to a situation, the results were beyond your expectations?

## Prayer

*You have blessed all generations, O God most high, in Jesus, our compassionate saviour, for through him you invite us to your kingdom, welcome us to your table, and provide us with nourishment in abundance.*

*Teach us to imitate your unfailing kindness and to build up Christ's body, the Church, by generously handing on to others the gifts we have received from your bounty. We ask this through our Lord Jesus Christ, your Son, who lives and reigns with you in the unity of the Holy Spirit, God for ever and ever. Amen.*

## ❧ Second Reading ❧

**1 Cor 11:23** For I received from the Lord what I also passed on to you, that the Lord Jesus on the night in which he was betrayed took bread, <sup>24</sup> and after he had given thanks he broke it and said, 'This is my body, which is for you. Do this in remembrance of me.' <sup>25</sup> In the same way, he also took the cup after supper, saying, 'This cup is the new covenant in my blood. Do this, every time you drink it, in remembrance of me.' <sup>26</sup> For every time you eat this bread and drink the cup, you proclaim the Lord's death until he comes.

### Initial observations

This reading – from the Mass of the Lord's Supper on Holy Thursday – is perfectly suitable for Corpus Christi. It is good to remember the more 'historical' context as we mark a 'doctrinal' feast, because our understanding of Eucharistic presence cannot be separated from the

Eucharist as whole, nor, indeed, from the contexts in the life of Jesus and in the practice of the early church.

## Kind of writing

Although within a letter, the excerpt is kind of *chreia*, or brief anecdote about Jesus. The Lord's Supper is reported four times in the New Testament, in the three Synoptic Gospels and here in Paul. Already divergences of tradition are apparent: Matthew and Mark represent one tradition while Luke and Paul represent another. All four versions are influenced by Christian practice subsequent to the Last Supper. Finally, Paul's version is the earliest to come down to us, but even there the telling is shaped by emerging liturgical practice. For example, it seems reasonable to suppose that the instruction to do this in remembrance (significantly absent in Matthew and Mark) represents a kind of later rubric or liturgical catechesis rather than words spoken by the historical Jesus.

## Origin of the reading

The context in the community is provided by Paul himself. According to the apostle's teaching, social distinctions – whether based on nature and gender, or socially constructed – have no place in the Christian polity. Paul has already signalled this in the letter: *For in the one Spirit we were all baptised into one body – Jews or Greeks, slaves or free – and we were all made to drink of one Spirit* (1 Corinthians 12:13; cf. Galatians 3:28).

There are two things to bear in mind. (i) The Corinthian church was not one but was divided into several house churches. (ii) At this early stage, the Lord's Supper had not become detached from the regular evening dinner. In the highly stratified society of the day, it is no surprise that social distinctions re-emerged in a quite ugly way (see 1 Corinthians 11:17–22 below). Paul is quite stern with them.

It looks as if the Lord's Supper took place in two moments. The words over the bread were spoken during the dinner (the *deipnon*) proper while the words over the cup were spoken during the subsequent drinks party (the symposium). Presumably, some were free to come on time while others, perhaps a lower class, did not enjoy the same flexibility. Hence, Paul's attack: *one goes hungry and another becomes drunk.* The Pauline vision of inclusion without distinction is rooted in the teaching and practice of Jesus himself. Any exclusion is in tension with the proclamation of the kingdom and the burden of proof rests with those who would exclude. The issue at stake is a combination of vision, values and practice. Paul's interim solution is disarmingly practical and direct: *So then, my brothers and sisters, when you come together to eat, wait for one another. If you are hungry, eat at home, so that when you come together, it will not be for your condemnation. About the other things I will give instructions when I come.* In other words, if you are that hungry, have a sandwich! (1 Corinthians 11:33–34).

## Related passages

> Now in the following instructions I do not commend you, because when you come together it is not for the better but for the worse. For, to begin with, when you come together as a church, I hear that there are divisions among you; and to some extent I believe it. Indeed, there have to be factions among you, for only so will it become clear who among you are genuine. When you come together, it is not really to eat the Lord's supper. For when the time comes to eat, each of you goes ahead with your own supper, and one goes hungry and another becomes drunk. What! Do you not have homes to eat and drink in? Or do you show contempt for the church of God and humiliate those who have nothing? What should I say to you? Should I commend you? In this matter I do not commend you! (1 Corinthians 11:17–22)

> Welcome one another, therefore, just as Christ has welcomed you, for the glory of God. For I tell you that Christ has become a servant of the circumcised on behalf of the truth of God in order that he might confirm the promises given to the patriarchs, and in order that the Gentiles might glorify God for his mercy. (Romans 15:7–9)

## Brief commentary

(V. 23)

The language used – received, passed on – reflects technical rabbinic terms for passing down a tradition. 'Betrayed' is probably not a good translation choice here. The term means literally 'handed over', and in the Pauline writing God is the implied subject. Again, the Greek reads *artos*, meaning bread, loaf, food. The NRSV correctly expands it into 'a loaf of bread' precisely because *there is one bread, we who are many are one body, for we all partake of the one bread* (1 Corinthians 10:17).

(V. 24)

Historically, the words and actions constitute a prophetic gesture intended to interpret the meaning of Jesus' death the following day. It is likely that the instruction to repeat comes from the tradition available to both Paul and Luke. Remembrance (*zikkron*) is used in the strong Jewish sense of effective memorial.

(V. 25)

Notice 'after the supper', reflecting Graeco-Roman meal practices, according to which drinks followed the food. Jesus associates his death with the covenant and with prophetic hopes for a new covenant. Blood represents the principle of life within a person and points to his giving of his whole being.

(V. 26)

This verse is no pious exclamation but rather takes us to the heart of the matter. In Paul's teaching, the death of Jesus was God's extraordinary gesture of compassionate solidarity with broken humanity, a solidarity so deep that all the distinctions we experience – both natural and constructed – are radically set aside. Thus, the issue at Corinth was not simply practical or moral but rather it touched the heart of the Christian proclamation, in faith and in life. If we really believed this, our practice would indeed be radically other.

## Pointers for prayer

a) Can I recall a time when the deep meaning of the Eucharist struck home?

b) If I were asked to say a few words about the Eucharist, what would I say?

c) What do I miss when I cannot, for whatever reason, take part in the Eucharist?

## Prayer

*Send into our hearts, O Lord, your Holy Spirit, that we may truly recognise all as our brothers and sisters in the breaking of the bread. Through Christ our Lord. Amen.*

## 🍃 First Reading 🍃

**Genesis 14:17** *After his return from the defeat of Chedorlaomer and the kings who were with him, the king of Sodom went out to meet him at the Valley of Shaveh (that is, the King's Valley).*

[18] And King Melchizedek of Salem brought out bread and wine; he was priest of God Most High. [19] He blessed him and said,

'Blessed be Abram by God Most High,
    maker of heaven and earth;
[20] and blessed be God Most High,
    who has delivered your enemies
into your hand!'

And Abram gave him one tenth of everything. [21] *Then the king of Sodom said to Abram, 'Give me the persons, but take the goods for yourself.'* [22] *But Abram said to the king of Sodom, 'I have sworn to the Lord, God Most High, maker of heaven and earth,* [23] *that I would not take a thread or a sandal-thong or anything that is yours, so that you might not say, 'I have made Abram rich.'* [24] *I will take nothing but what the young men have eaten, and the share of the men who went with me – Aner, Eshcol and Mamre. Let them take their share.'*

## Initial observations

The superficial link with the feast is the mention of bread and wine. There is, of course, a much deeper connection, familiar from the Letter to the Hebrews, that we can explore in these reflections.

## Kind of writing

With this unique appearance, Melchizedek is a bit of a mystery figure, giving rise to a great deal of speculation later on. The king is an otherwise unknown figure and even 'Salem' is unknown. Within the full story, the generosity of the king of Salem is contrasted with the lack of generosity of the king of Sodom.

In Qumran, Melchizedek was a source of further speculation and evolution, with even one document dedicated to him, 1QMelch. He enjoys both a high place in heaven and a role in eschatological judgement.

Hebrews exploits Melchizedek as eternal high priest of mysterious origin and issue: *Without father, without mother, without genealogy, having neither beginning of days nor end of life, but resembling the Son of God, he remains a priest for ever* (Hebrews 7:3). See also Psalm 110.

## Origin of the reading

The book of Genesis is made up of two large sections, as follows:

*Primeval History*
Genesis 1: origin of the world
Genesis 2–11: origin of the nations

*Origin of Israel*
Genesis 12–25 the Abraham cycle
Genesis 26–36 the Jacob cycle
Genesis 36–50 the Joseph cycle

Our reading comes from early in the Abraham cycle of tales.

The full scene (vv.17–24) is carefully choreographed:

v. 17 King of Sodom arrives     A
v. 18 King of Salem arrives     B
vv. 19–20 King of Salem speaks   B*
v. 21 King of Sodom speaks     A*
vv. 22–24 Abraham replies

In the context of the time of writing, this encounter is meant to legitimise the Jerusalem priesthood as ancient (predating Abraham's arrival) and centred in the holy city from time immemorial. Very likely, the priests of the time of writing are staking a claim over against the 'secular' rulers of Judah under the Persians.

## Related passages

> Then one who had escaped came and told Abram the Hebrew, who was living by the oaks of Mamre the Amorite, brother of Eshcol and of Aner; these were allies of Abram. When Abram heard that his nephew had been taken captive, he led forth his trained men, born in his house, three hundred eighteen of them, and went in pursuit as far as Dan. He divided his forces against them by night, he and his servants, and routed them and pursued them to Hobah, north of Damascus. Then he brought back all the goods, and also brought back his nephew Lot with his goods, and the women and the people. (Genesis 14:13–16) (vv. 17–24 as above)

> The LORD has sworn and will not change his mind, 'You are a priest for ever according to the order of Melchizedek.' (Psalm 110:4)

## Brief commentary

(V. 18)

Both kings met Abraham simultaneously, so that this vignette is not really a separate episode. The etymology of the name is important in later tradition and in Hebrews. It means either Milku-is-righteous (a person) or My king-is-righteous (in general). When Hebrews reads Salem to mean *shalom*, this is a rather forced, even historically false derivation, serving a theological purpose. Salem is unknown. Bread and wine are royal fare in the ancient Near East (1 Samuel 16:20) and often accompany animal sacrifice (Numbers 15:2–10; 1 Samuel 1:24; 10:3). In any case, Melchizedek is putting on a royal feast for the conquering Abraham. 'God Most High' translates accurately El-Elyon, one of the divine titles used by the patriarchs: El means the Deity and Elyon means Most High.

(Vv. 19–20)

In the next two verses the word 'to bless' is heard. Cf. Now the Lord said to Abram, 'Go from your country and your kindred and your father's house to the land that I will show you. I will make of you a great nation, and I will bless you, and make your name great, so that you will be a blessing. I will bless those who bless you, and the one who curses you I will curse; and in you all the families of the earth shall be blessed' (Genesis 12:1–3). Tithing was a widespread custom in the ancient Near East. Thus Abraham responds to the gesture of Melchizedek and also sets an example (!) for his descendants.

## Pointers for prayer

a) Have you experienced being blessed by God and felt the call to be a source of blessing?

b) God, the most high creator, is also a lover who loves and guides the lives of us all. How do you see God's presence and action in your life?

## Prayer

*Loving God, your door is always open, your table always spread. Show us how to be hospitable and welcoming, for by so doing we may entertain angels unawares. Through Christ our Lord. Amen.*

## Themes across the readings

It is good, outside the intensity of Holy Week, to have time to reflect on what we are doing when we 'do' Eucharist. Perhaps the traditional isolation of the Lord's Eucharistic presence from the action of the Eucharist represented a kind of distortion. We know today that Eucharist really is something we 'do' together: we bring, we bless, we break and we eat together. Even more, we recognise the body of Christ as we receive into our lives all those around the table. The experience and teaching of Paul is as relevant today as it was all those centuries ago in Corinth.

# On Being a Synodal Church

## The Church needs fixing

For the Catholic Church in Ireland, the times are critical as never before. Let me name four dimensions that stand out for me. Firstly, with all the good will in the world, handing on the faith to the next generation has not 'worked' for several decades, for two, if not three generations. The current practice of the sacraments of initiation is a cultural shell, colourful but empty. Secondly, we carry a history that makes it clear that the Church has not always been a force for good. Thirdly, we must take up the challenge of the role of women in the Church. We, as organisation, need the participation and voice of women throughout the Church, at all levels, including government and ministry. This is often seen as a question of justice. More fundamentally, it means fulfilling the Gospel vision. St Paul put it thus:

> As many of you as were baptised into Christ have clothed yourselves with Christ. There is no longer Jew or Greek, there is no longer slave or free, there is no longer male and female; for all of you are one in Christ Jesus. (Galatians 3:27–28)

Finally, as we face the imminent collapse of the ordained ministry, the roles and responsibilities of the laity will have to be reviewed and reformed, theologically and canonically. Taken together, these four issues portray a context critical as never before. You can't beat a good crisis and the opportunity should not be wasted, as Churchill reputedly said.

### Pope Francis: A synodal pathway

By the grace of God, Pope Francis has initiated a worldwide consultation of all Catholics in a vast process, leading to a national synod in all countries and an international synod in Rome. The word synod comes from two Greek words: *syn* + *hodos*. *Hodos* means a way or road, and *syn* means with. So a synod is a journey we make together. Synod and synodality are not quite the same. A synod is the actual gathering. Synodality points not so much to an event but indicates a participative way of being church, a whole way of looking at things that ought to characterise our journey together into the future.

There have always been synods in the course of Church history, so in one sense this is quite traditional. However, nothing quite like this hoped-for participation of all the parishes and all the baptised has ever occurred before. This way of doing synod and being church, under the thin guise of tradition, is radically new. What all this means should not be underestimated. The Second Vatican Council proclaimed that the Church is first of all the people of God, all the baptised together. This new synodal process is a re-awakening of that vision – in my own mind it is leading to a kind of Third Vatican Council.

Theologians used to joke about what might follow the Second Vatican Council. Given the prominence of the bishops at the Second Vatican Council, who would be taking the lead at the third or even fourth councils? Our potential 'Third Vatican Council' turns out to be the people of God and the bishops. The Spirit can still surprise, thanks be to God.

The synodal pathway is guided by a key question: what does God desire of his Church today? In a word, how can we as a community of faith offer the word of life, the Gospel, in our time? And, accordingly, how should we so organise and structure ourselves so that we can more adequately serve that greater vision?

Pope Francis knows and loves his Bible. It is interesting to see what inspires him when he searches the Scriptures. The obvious story for a synod would have been the council of Jerusalem (Acts 15:1–35), resembling, as it does, in some fashion our synodal journey. However, the chosen story is that of Cornelius in Acts 10:1–11:18, to which we shall now devote our attention.

## Inspiration: Acts 10:1–11:18

The Acts of the Apostles offers itself as a history, covering the period from the death and resurrection of Jesus to just before the death of St Paul. In a rough calculation, this means a thirty-five-year period. The author has no pretensions to comprehensiveness, trying to tell *all* that happened. On the contrary, in the twenty-eight chapters of Acts, the writer both selects and repeats stories. An example would be Pentecost itself. The major occurrence in Acts 2:1–13 is both synthetic and programmatic. It gathers in foundational experiences of the Spirit and writes the account in the light of the Tower of Babel (Genesis 11:1–9) and the Jewish harvest festival of Shavuot or Pentecost (see Chapter 9 of this volume). It is also programmatic because Pentecost, reassuringly, continues, and there are further aftershocks or 'pentecosts' in Acts 8:14–17; 10:44–46; 19:1–7. The so-called conversion of St Paul is recounted no fewer than three times (Acts 9:1–31; 22:1–21; 26:2-23). The writer chooses to do the same with the story of Cornelius, a story that is the foundational experience leading to the council of Jerusalem in Acts 15. Repetition is the hallmark of the story of Cornelius. This 'map' may help.

| Verses | Actors | Agents | Place | Content |
|---|---|---|---|---|
| 10:1–8 | Cornelius | An angel | Caesarea | To send for Peter |
| 10 :9–16 | Peter | Lord | Joppa | All foods are clean |
| 10:17–23 | Messengers and Peter | A holy angel | Joppa | Vision recounted |
| 10:24–33 | Cornelius and Peter | God; a 'man' in dazzling robes | Caesarea | Visions recounted |
| 10:34–43 | Peter's speech | Holy Spirit | Caesarea | God is impartial |
| 10:44–48 | Mini-Pentecost | Holy Spirit | Caesarea | Baptism |
| 11:1–18 | Peter | The Lord; an angel; the Holy Spirit | Jerusalem | Both visions repeated |

The importance of this episode for the whole project of Acts is evident from the sheer density of repetition. Cornelius first appears in Acts 10:1–8. That same story is recounted three more times in Acts in 10:11–16 (Peter), 10:17–23 (the messengers) and 10:30–33 (Cornelius). In a similar way, the experience of Peter on the roof is first given in Acts 10:9–16. The vision of the contraption with all the creatures on it is, naturally, told three times at this point and then the whole account is rehearsed once more in Jerusalem (Acts 11:2–10), again in threefold fashion. The mini-Pentecost in Acts 10:44–48 is then retold in Jerusalem (Acts 11:15–17). The episode as such is interpreted by the speech of Peter in Acts 10:34–43, a speech interrupted by the irruption of the Holy Spirit. The key question is asked by Peter: 'Can anyone withhold the water for baptising these people who have received the Holy Spirit just as we have?' (Acts 10:47). As we might expect, this rhetorical question is repeated in different words in Acts 11:17. What may surprise the contemporary reader is the bestowal of the Holy Spirit *before* baptism, *ahead* of aggregation to the community of believers. Baptism becomes almost the formal recognition of a fait accompli. In case we may still have managed to overlook the significance of this sequence, the core insight that 'God has made no distinction between them and us' finds a final iteration at the council of Jerusalem in Acts 15:7–14.

There are two other features of the story which are quietly revealing. In the preceding chapter, we are told that Peter was staying at the house of Simon the tanner (Acts 9:43). At first glance, it seems unexceptional. Simon is Jewish with a typically Jewish name. His line of work was the problem. According to Leviticus 11:39–43, a tanner is *perpetually* unclean. In the later Rabbinic tradition, the following observations are made: a father ought not to teach his son to be a tanner; it was easier for a tanner's wife to get a divorce; a synagogue could not be sold for use as a tannery; a tannery could not be within fifty cubits from a town. The throwaway remark about Simon *the tanner* indicates that Peter already thought that the purity laws did not apply to Jews or to those who associate with them.

Cornelius, we are told, was praying at three o'clock in the afternoon (Acts 10:3), an hour already noticed in Acts 3:1. Again, an incidental detail is revealing. Cornelius, in pagan Caesarea, had aligned his prayer with the prayer times in the Temple in Jerusalem. He is what was called an authentic God-fearer, a person of Gentile origin attracted to Judaism on account of its evident antiquity, its pure monotheism and its superior ethics. Just as Peter had already made a journey from the centre to the edges, Cornelius had made a journey from the edges to the centre.

When we read the whole story again carefully, a few key insights emerge. The first of these concerns the Holy Spirit. The Holy Spirit – the chief protagonist in the Acts – is unpredictable and always ahead of us. The Spirit is not confined by the boundaries humans have established, then or now. We may note, finally, the struggle experienced by the believers attend to the working of the Spirit: Peter, the Jerusalem community and the council of Jerusalem all experienced significant resistance. This is our experience too.

Traditionally, the name for this story is the conversion of Cornelius, one of at least ten such stories in the Acts (2:1–47; 3:1–4:4, 32–37; 8:4–25; 8:26–40; 9:1–31; 10:1–48; 13:6–12; 13:13–52; 16:11–15; 16:25–34). Cornelius certainly underwent a conversion, as part of a longer journey of faith and devotion. But there are two other conversions. Initially, Peter himself experienced a somewhat laborious conversion by means of the vision with its contraption. In our day, we may miss the meaning. Declaring all foods clean meant that full table-fellowship with Gentiles is now possible. Initially, Peter was faithful and resistant, until he realised that it was God the creator who was speaking to him. Thirdly, the community of believers in Jerusalem, perhaps more homogenous, seemed surprised that Gentiles accepted the word of God. The closing verse is both elliptical and lucid: When they heard this, they were silenced. And they praised God, saying, 'Then God has given even to the Gentiles the repentance that leads to life' (Acts 11:18). The central conversion was not that of one more Gentile but that of Peter and the church in Jerusalem. Perhaps God has in mind further conversions for the Church in our day?

Why was this journey of inclusion so laboured? The wider inclusion of the Gentiles in the Christian way has left its mark in the Acts, Mark, Matthew and John, but also in the earlier Romans and Galatians. Why was this such a struggle, when it seems so obvious to us? The key here is that the early church had no guidance on this matter from Jesus himself. The historical Jesus met almost no Gentiles. Of the few stories we have, some are not properly historical. In other words, the issue of table-fellowship with Gentiles did not arise during the ministry. Much less did the issue of circumcision, which so exercised St Paul. Now we can understand why nobody, not even James, ever appealed to the teaching of Jesus, which would surely have clinched such a discussion.

The attentive Bible reader may object, but what about Mark 7, where we read: Thus he declared all foods clean (Mark 7:19)? With many other scholars, I think Mark 7:17–23 represents a retrojection onto the historical Jesus of an insight and teaching that come from the early Church. Mark had no follow-up history of the Church, so he had to place the story within the ministry of Jesus and he did so in a very significant context in his gospel, between the two multiplications of the loaves. We may note, in passing, that Luke omits this part of Mark in his rewriting of the First Gospel.

So, we come to an interesting conclusion. The early believers found themselves in a new situation, they had no teaching or precedent from Jesus to go on, so they just had to work it out for themselves. *How* they did that is preserved in Acts 15:1–35. From that account we see that every side was listened to; the Cornelius story was remembered; the work of the Spirit was received; the Scriptures were read; a principle was established not to add any burden. In the end, a compromise was reached to allow full table-fellowship between Jews and Gentiles. Surprisingly, the Jews were willing – seemingly – to set aside both the sabbath and circumcision, but could not bring themselves to eat meat with blood still in it. A sensible, practical and probably short-term compromise was agreed and the Gentiles were asked to be flexible and generous.

The story of Cornelius, the foundation for Acts 15, proves instructive for today. In the many issues before us, we are in a situation not dissimilar to that of the early church. We have no teaching from Jesus to go on and so we have to work things out for ourselves by hearing everyone out, by noticing the work of the Spirit, by reading the Scriptures, by choosing not to impose needless burdens. In the end, there may be some compromises so we can all stay in communion.

The purposeful choice of this passage by Pope Francis was surely inspired and, for us, inspiring, as we undertake our synodal pathway into the future.

## Will it work?

A blunt question can be asked: will this work? Well, first of all, this is new and mistakes will be made and shortcomings will be evident. So far, so normal. Nevertheless, we all learn by doing, as Aristotle said so long ago. In Europe, this whole process might seem quite theoretical, even idealistic. But in South America, such a synodal church has operated already for several decades. It is no accident that the present bishop of Rome comes from Argentina – he has lived this synodal Church first of all at home.

In South America, they have a wealth of practical experience and expertise on what is involved. Even so, no doubt they also fall short. (Welcome to the human race, will you be staying long?). But at least there is experience on the ground which shows that a participative Church is the only way forward. Also, let us also not forget to place our trust in the Holy Spirit – always ahead of us, always full of surprises.

## What to do now?

A final consideration. What can I do now? We can all do at least three things immediately. First of all, become informed about what is happening. This can be done on the diocesan websites. On the Dublin one, you will find an easy-to-understand presentation called 'Simply Synod'. Secondly, begin to pray for the synodal process. There is an official prayer, 'We stand before you, Holy Spirit', but there is also a choice of prayers. We should keep this whole adventure in our prayer that the Spirit may indeed guide us and that we might listen to what the Spirit is saying to the churches. Thirdly, when the opportunity arises, especially at parish level, let your voice be heard. Don't hesitate to take part – the synodal pathway will work only if we all take the risk of getting involved.

It is also not forbidden to become excited. Who knows where the

Spirit will take us? After a long period of struggle and difficulty, stagnation and disappointment, here at last we have good news – something wonderful is happening. We could permit ourselves to become excited.

*Soli Deo Gloria!*

# Biblical Index

The index follows the order of Old Testament books as found in Catholic Bibles; the chapter and verse numbering follows the NRSV.

**Other ancient sources**